Theory & Application of LLM Model: Create Intelligent Apps and Agents with Large Language Models

By K.Khan

Table of Contents

Introduction

The field of artificial intelligence is undergoing a profound transformation, with Large Language Models (LLMs) at the forefront of this revolution. These models, powered by billions of parameters, have demonstrated an unprecedented ability to generate human-like text, answer complex queries, and perform tasks that were once considered the exclusive domain of human intelligence. This book is your gateway to understanding and harnessing the power of LLMs to create intelligent applications and agents that can transform industries and redefine user experiences.

As AI technologies evolve, LLMs are emerging as a cornerstone for building sophisticated applications, ranging from chatbots and virtual assistants to recommendation systems and coding tools. However, leveraging their potential requires more than just technical know-how; it demands a structured approach to understanding, integrating, and optimizing these models within your projects.

In this book, you will embark on a step-by-step journey that will guide you through every facet of developing LLM-powered applications. From choosing the right model and engineering effective prompts to fine-tuning and deploying your solutions responsibly, this guide provides comprehensive insights and practical examples to help you succeed.

Whether you are a developer, data scientist, AI engineer, or an enthusiast eager to explore the world of LLMs, this book is designed to equip you with the knowledge and skills needed to build intelligent systems that push the boundaries of innovation. Let us begin this exciting journey into the realm of Large Language Models and discover how they can transform ideas into reality.

Preface

The advent of Large Language Models (LLMs) has revolutionized the landscape of artificial intelligence, opening doors to unprecedented possibilities. These models have reshaped how we interact with technology, enabling the creation of applications that were once considered science fiction. This book was born out of the growing need for a comprehensive, practical guide that bridges the gap between theoretical knowledge and real-world implementation of LLM-powered applications.

The journey of writing this book has been driven by a singular goal: to empower readers with the tools and understanding they need to leverage LLMs effectively. From developers looking to build conversational AI systems to data scientists aiming to enhance analytics workflows, this book provides step-by-step guidance tailored for diverse audiences. The content is enriched with insights drawn from hands-on experience, ensuring its relevance and applicability.

What sets this book apart is its emphasis on practicality. We delve into not only the "how" but also the "why" behind each concept, enabling you to make informed decisions as you design, develop, and deploy LLM-powered solutions. Each chapter builds upon the last, gradually introducing complexity while maintaining clarity, making this book a valuable resource for both beginners and seasoned professionals.

We also recognize the importance of responsibility in AI development. As LLMs become more prevalent, addressing ethical considerations, biases, and fairness becomes paramount. This book dedicates an entire chapter to Responsible AI, reflecting our commitment to fostering a future where AI is both innovative and ethical.

We hope this book serves as a catalyst for your creative and technical aspirations, inspiring you to push the boundaries of what is possible with LLMs. Thank you for joining us on this exciting journey into the world of intelligent applications and agents. Let's explore, innovate, and build together!

Chapter 1: Introduction to Large Language Models

What Are Large Language Models (LLMs)?

Large Language Models (LLMs) are a class of artificial intelligence systems designed to understand and generate human-like text. These models are trained on vast amounts of data, encompassing diverse topics, languages, and writing styles. At their core, LLMs predict the next word in a sequence based on the context of the preceding words, enabling them to generate coherent and contextually relevant responses.

LLMs, such as OpenAI's GPT-4 and Google's BERT, have revolutionized natural language processing (NLP) by achieving state-of-the-art performance in tasks like translation, summarization, and question-answering. Their ability to comprehend and produce text with remarkable fluency makes them invaluable tools for building intelligent applications.

Key features of LLMs include:

- **Contextual Understanding**: LLMs grasp the nuances of language, considering the context of entire paragraphs or documents.
- **Versatility**: They can perform a wide range of tasks, from creative writing to technical analysis.
- **Scalability**: LLMs can handle vast datasets and generate high-quality responses in real-time.

Evolution of LLMs: From GPT to GPT-4 and Beyond

The journey of LLMs began with simple language models that relied on rule-based or statistical techniques. The advent of deep learning transformed this field, giving rise to neural networks capable of learning intricate patterns in text data. Let's explore the key milestones:

1. **GPT (Generative Pre-trained Transformer)**: OpenAI introduced GPT, a model pre-trained on extensive datasets and fine-tuned for specific tasks. It laid the foundation for subsequent advancements.
2. **GPT-2**: With an increased parameter count, GPT-2 demonstrated unprecedented language generation capabilities, sparking debates about the ethical implications of such powerful models.
3. **GPT-3**: Boasting 175 billion parameters, GPT-3 marked a leap forward, enabling applications like chatbots, content creation, and coding assistance.
4. **GPT-4 and Beyond**: The evolution continues, focusing on multimodal capabilities, reduced biases, and improved efficiency.

Key Features and Capabilities of LLMs

LLMs excel in several areas, including:

- **Text Generation**: Crafting essays, stories, and reports with minimal input.
- **Question Answering**: Providing accurate answers to queries based on context.
- **Translation**: Converting text between languages with high accuracy.
- **Sentiment Analysis**: Determining the emotional tone of text.

The Role of LLMs in Modern AI Systems

LLMs serve as the backbone of numerous AI-powered systems, enabling functionalities that were once the realm of human expertise. From powering virtual assistants to driving personalized marketing campaigns, their impact is profound and far-reaching.

By understanding the foundations of LLMs, you'll be better equipped to harness their potential in your projects. The subsequent chapters will delve into practical applications, guiding you through the process of building innovative and impactful solutions.

Chapter 2: LLMs for AI-Powered Applications

Large Language Models (LLMs) are not just theoretical constructs; they are transforming industries and redefining how we approach problem-solving in the digital age. This chapter explores the practical applications of LLMs across various sectors, emphasizing their business value and showcasing real-world examples.

2.1 Real-World Applications of LLMs

LLMs' versatility enables them to address diverse use cases, including but not limited to:

2.1.1 Customer Support

- **Chatbots and Virtual Assistants**: LLMs power intelligent chatbots like OpenAI's ChatGPT, enabling businesses to provide 24/7 customer support. These bots can handle FAQs, resolve issues, and escalate complex problems to human agents.
- **Benefits**: Reduced response times, increased customer satisfaction, and lower operational costs.

2.1.2 Content Creation

- **Blog and Article Writing**: LLMs assist in generating high-quality content tailored to specific audiences. Tools like Jasper AI utilize LLMs to help marketers and writers.
- **Ad Copywriting**: AI-powered platforms create engaging advertisements, optimizing them for target demographics.

2.1.3 Healthcare

- **Clinical Documentation**: LLMs can transcribe and summarize patient-doctor interactions, reducing administrative burdens on healthcare professionals.
- **Patient Education**: Chatbots powered by LLMs provide information about medications, treatments, and preventive care in an easily digestible format.

2.1.4 Education

- **Personalized Learning**: LLMs customize learning experiences by analyzing a student's progress and providing tailored exercises.
- **Automated Grading**: They grade essays and assignments, offering constructive feedback.

- **Code Assistance**: Developers use LLM-powered tools like GitHub Copilot to autocomplete code, debug errors, and suggest improvements.
- **Documentation Generation**: LLMs create comprehensive API documentation, saving developers hours of manual work.

2.2 Transforming Industries with LLMs

2.2.1 E-commerce

- **Personalized Recommendations**: LLMs analyze user behavior to suggest products, enhancing the shopping experience.
- **Intelligent Search**: They improve search accuracy by understanding user intent and contextualizing queries.

2.2.2 Finance

- **Fraud Detection**: LLMs identify anomalies in transaction data, flagging potential fraud.
- **Customer Support**: Virtual assistants help users manage accounts, check balances, and understand financial products.

2.2.3 Media and Entertainment

- **Scriptwriting**: LLMs generate storylines and dialogues for films, TV shows, and video games.
- **Subtitling and Dubbing**: They produce accurate subtitles and assist in dubbing content into multiple languages.

2.3 The Business Value of LLMs

Investing in LLM-powered applications provides tangible benefits:

2.3.1 Enhanced Efficiency

Automation reduces manual effort, allowing organizations to allocate resources to higher-value tasks.

By streamlining operations, businesses can lower overhead costs, such as staffing for customer support or manual content creation.

2.3.3 Improved User Experience

LLMs enable highly responsive and personalized interactions, fostering customer loyalty.

2.3.4 Competitive Advantage

Adopting cutting-edge AI technologies positions companies as industry leaders, attracting both customers and investors.

2.4 Case Studies of Successful LLM Deployments

2.4.1 OpenAI and Duolingo

- **Scenario**: Duolingo integrated OpenAI's GPT-4 to create AI-driven language learning features.
- **Outcome**: The platform now offers more personalized exercises and realistic conversation practice, enhancing user engagement.

2.4.2 Shopify's AI Chatbots

- **Scenario**: Shopify employed LLM-powered chatbots to assist merchants in setting up and managing online stores.
- **Outcome**: The bots reduced onboarding time and improved merchant satisfaction.

2.4.3 Legal Research with Casetext

- **Scenario**: Casetext uses LLMs to analyze legal documents and case law, helping lawyers prepare for trials more efficiently.
- **Outcome**: Time spent on research decreased by up to 50%, allowing lawyers to focus on strategy.

Practical Tips for Identifying LLM Use Cases

1. **Analyze Pain Points**: Identify repetitive, time-consuming tasks that could benefit from automation.

2. **Consider Scalability**: Focus on use cases where LLMs can scale solutions to a broader audience.
3. **Validate Feasibility**: Assess the availability of data and alignment of LLM capabilities with business objectives.
4. **Prototype and Test**: Develop proof-of-concept applications to gauge their effectiveness before full-scale deployment.

With these insights, you're now familiar with the transformative potential of LLMs across industries. The next chapter will guide you through choosing the right LLM for your specific application, ensuring your project aligns with technical and business requirements.

Chapter 3: Choosing an LLM for Your Application

Selecting the right Large Language Model (LLM) is a crucial step in the development of AI-powered applications. With numerous models available, understanding their strengths, weaknesses, and suitability for your use case is essential for maximizing performance and cost-effectiveness.

Key Factors to Consider

1. Accuracy and Performance

The effectiveness of an LLM often depends on its accuracy and ability to perform the tasks required for your application. Consider:

- **Language Understanding**: Does the model comprehend the nuances and intricacies of your target language(s)?
- **Task-Specific Performance**: Evaluate benchmarks like BLEU for translation or F1 scores for question-answering tasks relevant to your application.

Practical Example: Suppose you're building a customer support chatbot. Test the model's accuracy on a dataset of frequently asked questions (FAQs) and measure its ability to provide concise, relevant answers.

2. Scalability and Latency

Scalability and response time are critical for real-time applications.

- **Model Size**: Larger models may provide better accuracy but could also lead to higher latency.
- **Deployment Environment**: Assess whether the model will run on the cloud, edge devices, or in hybrid setups.

Practical Example: If you're developing an AI assistant for mobile devices, prioritize a lightweight model like OpenAI's GPT-3.5-turbo over GPT-4 for faster responses.

3. Cost

Balancing cost and performance is essential, especially for applications with high traffic or frequent usage.

- **Compute Costs**: Larger models require more computational resources.
- **Licensing Fees**: Proprietary models like OpenAI's GPT come with usage fees, while open-source alternatives may offer more cost-effective options.

Practical Example: For a small-scale educational app, consider using open-source models like Bloom or LLaMA to minimize operational expenses.

Open-Source vs. Proprietary LLMs

Open-Source LLMs

Open-source models offer flexibility and control. You can fine-tune and deploy them without usage restrictions.

- **Advantages**:
  - Cost-effective
  - Customizable
  - No dependency on external APIs
- **Challenges**:
  - Requires infrastructure for deployment
  - Performance may lag behind proprietary models

Popular Options:

- **Hugging Face Transformers**: Provides a library of pre-trained models.
- **GPT-Neo**: OpenAI's free alternative for lightweight tasks.

Practical Example: A startup with limited budget but strong technical expertise can use Hugging Face's DistilBERT for document summarization.

Proprietary LLMs

Proprietary models come with support and state-of-the-art performance but at a higher cost.

- **Advantages**:
  - Cutting-edge accuracy
  - Ready-to-use APIs
  - Scalable cloud solutions
- **Challenges**:
  - Expensive usage fees
  - Vendor lock-in risk

Popular Options:

- **OpenAI (GPT-4)**
- **Anthropic (Claude)**

Practical Example: A large enterprise looking for advanced chatbot features and reliability might choose OpenAI's GPT-4 with a managed API.

A Comparative Analysis of Popular LLMs

Model	Strengths	Limitations	Best Use Cases
OpenAI GPT-4	State-of-the-art performance	High cost	High-end chatbots
Google BERT	Excellent for text classification	Limited generative capabilities	Search and sentiment analysis
Hugging Face Models	Cost-effective, customizable	Requires infrastructure	Summarization, NLU tasks
Anthropic Claude	Ethical AI focus, robust conversation	Fewer integrations	Customer service automation

Practical Example: An e-commerce platform might choose Anthropic's Claude for ethical AI customer support while using GPT-4 for complex product recommendations.

Aligning LLM Capabilities with Business Needs

1. Define Your Objectives

Clearly articulate the problem you aim to solve. Are you creating a conversational agent, automating document analysis, or enhancing search capabilities?

Practical Example: For a legal firm needing document review, prioritize models trained on legal datasets.

2. Evaluate Your Resources

Consider technical expertise, infrastructure, and budget. A robust internal team can manage open-source solutions, while proprietary APIs are better for plug-and-play scenarios.

Practical Example: A non-technical team at a healthcare startup could adopt OpenAI's API for quick deployment of a symptom-checking bot.

3. Test and Iterate

Conduct pilot tests with a few options before committing. Analyze metrics like accuracy, latency, and user satisfaction.

Practical Example: Run A/B testing with two LLMs in a live environment to measure user engagement for a news summarization app.

Conclusion

Choosing the right LLM involves balancing technical, operational, and business considerations. By thoroughly evaluating options and aligning them with your objectives, you can lay a strong foundation for developing impactful AI-powered applications. The next chapter will guide you through the art of prompt engineering—a critical skill for maximizing the performance of your chosen LLM.

Chapter 4: Prompt Engineering

Prompt engineering is a foundational skill for effectively utilizing large language models (LLMs). It involves crafting input prompts to guide the LLM's responses in a way that meets your specific objectives. In this chapter, we'll delve into the fundamentals of prompt engineering, techniques for optimization, and practical examples to help you master this essential skill.

Fundamentals of Prompt Engineering

LLMs rely on the input they receive to generate output. The quality and clarity of this input, referred to as the "prompt," significantly influence the model's response. A well-engineered prompt can:

- **Enhance Accuracy**: Reduce ambiguity and ensure relevant responses.
- **Increase Efficiency**: Minimize the need for extensive post-processing.
- **Expand Functionality**: Unlock creative and complex use cases.

Components of a Prompt

A prompt typically consists of:

1. **Context**: Background information or instructions to set the stage for the model.
2. **Task Specification**: A clear description of the desired output.
3. **Examples (Optional)**: Providing examples to demonstrate the desired structure or style.

For example:

```
You are an expert virtual assistant. Summarize the following article in one
paragraph:

[Insert article text here]
```

Writing Effective Prompts

1. Be Specific

Clearly define the task and avoid vague instructions. For example, instead of:

```
Summarize this article.
```

Use:

```
Summarize this article in one paragraph, focusing on the main arguments.
```

2. Use Constraints

Set boundaries to control the output. For instance:

```
Generate a five-line poem about nature in rhyming couplets.
```

3. Add Context

Providing context ensures the model understands the scenario. For example:

```
You are a data analyst. Explain the significance of the following trends in
simple terms:

[Insert trends here]
```

4. Leverage Examples

Demonstrate the desired response format:

```
Translate the following English sentence into French. Example:
English: How are you?
French: Comment ça va?

Sentence: What is your name?
```

Techniques for Improving Model Responses

1. Iterative Refinement

Start with a general prompt and refine it based on the response:

Initial Prompt:

```
Write about machine learning.
```

Refined Prompt:

```
Write a 200-word article introducing the basics of machine learning for
beginners.
```

2. Chain-of-Thought Prompting

Encourage the model to explain its reasoning step-by-step:

```
Solve this math problem step-by-step: If 3x + 5 = 20, what is x?
```

3. Use System Messages (For API Integrations)

Guide the model's behavior with system-level instructions:

```
You are a polite customer service representative. Respond to the following
query with empathy and professionalism.
```

Tools for Prompt Optimization

Several tools and platforms can help test and optimize prompts:

- **OpenAI Playground**: Experiment with prompts in a sandbox environment.
- **LangChain**: A framework for building applications powered by language models, offering prompt templates and chaining capabilities.
- **Prompt Engineering Guides**: Online resources and communities sharing effective prompt techniques.

Practical Examples

Example 1: Summarization

Input:

```
Summarize the following text in three sentences:

[Insert text here]
```

Response:

```
The text discusses the benefits of renewable energy, highlighting its role in
reducing carbon emissions and fostering sustainability. It emphasizes the
need for government incentives to accelerate adoption. The article concludes
with predictions about future trends in renewable energy technology.
```

Example 2: Question Answering

Input:

```
Based on the text provided, answer the following question: What are the main
benefits of renewable energy?
```

Response:

```
The main benefits of renewable energy are reducing carbon emissions,
promoting sustainability, and decreasing reliance on fossil fuels.
```

Example 3: Creative Writing

Input:

```
Write a short story about a robot discovering friendship.
```

Response:

In a bustling city, a delivery robot named Max realized its daily route felt incomplete. One day, it met a stray cat that followed it around. As days passed, their unlikely friendship blossomed, showing Max that even a machine could find companionship in the most unexpected ways.

Mastering prompt engineering is an iterative process. Experimentation and refinement are key to unlocking the full potential of LLMs. The next chapter will explore how to seamlessly embed LLMs within your applications, bridging the gap between model capabilities and real-world use cases.

Chapter 5: Embedding LLMs within Your Applications

Integrating large language models (LLMs) into your applications involves more than just calling an API. It requires thoughtful planning to ensure the model's capabilities align with your application's goals, technical infrastructure, and user experience requirements. In this chapter, we will cover how to integrate LLMs into applications, discuss architectural considerations, and provide best practices for successful implementation.

Integrating LLMs Using APIs

Most LLMs, including OpenAI's GPT models, are accessible via APIs. These APIs provide a convenient interface for sending text-based prompts and receiving responses.

Steps to Integration:

1. **API Key Authentication:** Obtain an API key from the LLM provider and securely store it.
2. **Designing Requests:** Structure requests to include the input prompt, desired output format, and other parameters such as temperature or max tokens.
3. **Handling Responses:** Parse the output and integrate it into your application's workflow.

For example, using Python:

```python
import openai

# Set up API key
openai.api_key = "your-api-key"

# Send a request
response = openai.Completion.create(
    model="text-davinci-003",
    prompt="Summarize the following text in one sentence: [Your text here]",
    max_tokens=50
)

# Extract and use the response
print(response["choices"][0]["text"].strip())
```

Architecting LLM-Powered Solutions

Integrating LLMs requires careful consideration of the application's architecture to ensure scalability, reliability, and responsiveness.

Key Components:

1. **Frontend:** User interface where inputs are gathered and outputs are displayed.
2. **Backend:** Processes API calls, manages data, and handles business logic.

3. **Model Layer:** Interface with the LLM API, including prompt creation and response handling.
4. **Database:** Store prompts, responses, and user data for analytics and personalization.

Best Practices for LLM Integration

1. Modular Design

Develop the integration as a modular component that can be easily updated or replaced without disrupting the entire application.

2. Caching Mechanisms

Implement caching for frequently requested prompts to reduce latency and API costs.

3. Monitoring and Logging

Track API usage, response times, and error rates to ensure smooth operation and identify potential issues.

4. Cost Management

Optimize token usage by keeping prompts concise and using lower-cost models for non-critical tasks.

Overcoming Integration Challenges

1. Handling Ambiguous Outputs

Mitigate ambiguity by refining prompts and validating responses using rule-based checks or additional LLM calls.

2. Managing Latency

Use asynchronous API calls and prioritize critical requests to minimize the impact of latency.

3. Scaling for High Demand

Distribute API requests across multiple instances and leverage rate-limiting strategies to handle spikes in traffic.

Embedding LLMs within your applications can significantly enhance functionality, but it requires a strategic approach. In the next chapter, we will dive into building conversational applications, focusing on creating intelligent, context-aware chatbots and virtual assistants.

Chapter 6: Building Conversational Applications

Introduction:

Conversational applications are among the most popular and impactful uses of Large Language Models (LLMs). These applications include chatbots, virtual assistants, and other dialogue systems capable of understanding and responding to human input in a meaningful way. In this chapter, we will explore the key components of conversational applications, techniques to build and optimize them, and practical examples to ensure robust and user-friendly interactions.

Designing Conversational Interfaces

A well-designed conversational interface is crucial for delivering a seamless and intuitive user experience. The key considerations are:

1. Understanding the User Journey

- **Identify Use Cases**: Define the purpose of the chatbot or virtual assistant. Is it for customer support, lead generation, or personal assistance?
- **User Goals**: Anticipate user intents, such as querying product details or scheduling appointments.
- **Conversation Flow**: Map out the flow of possible user interactions to ensure clarity and logical progression.

2. User Interface Design

- **Text Inputs and Outputs**: Provide a clean interface for users to type or speak their queries.
- **Fallback Options**: Include buttons or quick reply options for common actions.
- **Accessibility**: Ensure the interface supports diverse users, including those with disabilities.

Understanding Natural Language Understanding (NLU)

Natural Language Understanding is at the core of conversational applications. It involves interpreting user inputs and mapping them to relevant intents or actions.

Key Components of NLU:

1. **Intent Recognition**: Understanding the purpose behind user input.
   Example:
   - Input: *"I need to reset my password."*
   - Recognized Intent: *Password Reset*

2. **Entity Extraction**: Identifying key details within the input.
   Example:
   - ○ Input: *"Book a flight to New York tomorrow."*
   - ○ Extracted Entities: *Destination: New York, Date: Tomorrow*
3. **Context Maintenance**: Retaining information across turns in a conversation.
   Example:
   - ○ User: *"I need a hotel."*
   - ○ Bot: *"In which city?"*
   - ○ User: *"New York."*
   - ○ Context Maintained: *Hotel booking for New York.*

Implementing Dialogue Management Systems

Dialogue management involves controlling the flow of the conversation based on user input and application logic.

Techniques for Dialogue Management:

1. **Rule-Based Systems**:
   Predefined rules guide the conversation flow.
   Example: If intent is *"password reset"*, direct the user to the password reset page.
2. **State-Based Systems**:

   Track the conversation state to handle complex dialogues.

   Example:

   - State: User has provided destination but not date.
   - Prompt: *"What date would you like to travel?"*
   -
3. **Machine Learning-Based Systems**:

   Use models trained on conversation data to predict the next action. Example: Reinforcement learning models optimizing customer satisfaction.

Enhancing Chatbot Performance with LLMs

LLMs bring advanced capabilities to chatbots, such as understanding nuances, generating natural responses, and adapting to context.

1. Fine-Tuning for Domain-Specific Knowledge:

- Train the model on domain-specific datasets to improve accuracy.
- Example: A healthcare chatbot can be fine-tuned with medical FAQs to provide precise answers.

2. Dynamic Prompt Engineering:

- Create prompts that adapt based on user inputs.
- Example:
  - User Query: *"Tell me about my order status."*
  - Prompt: *"You are a customer support agent. The user asks about the status of their order. Respond politely using the order information provided: [Order Details]."*

3. Multi-Turn Conversations:

- Maintain context across multiple interactions.
- Example:
  - User: *"What's the weather in Paris?"*
  - Bot: *"It's sunny in Paris today."*
  - User: *"What about tomorrow?"*
  - Context Retained: *Weather inquiry for Paris.*

Practical Examples

Example 1: Customer Support Chatbot

Scenario: A chatbot for an e-commerce platform.

Implementation:

```
import openai

# API key setup
openai.api_key = "your-api-key"

# Define the conversation
def customer_support_chatbot(user_input):
    prompt = f"""
    You are a helpful customer service agent for an e-commerce platform.
Respond to the following query:
    {user_input}
    """
    response = openai.Completion.create(
        model="text-davinci-003",
        prompt=prompt,
        max_tokens=150
    )
```

```
        return response['choices'][0]['text'].strip()

# Test the chatbot
print(customer_support_chatbot("I want to return an item I purchased last
week."))
```

Example 2: Personal Assistant

Scenario: A personal assistant to schedule meetings.

Implementation:

```
def schedule_meeting(user_input):
    prompt = f"""
    You are a virtual assistant. The user says: '{user_input}'. Help them
schedule a meeting.
    """
    response = openai.Completion.create(
        model="text-davinci-003",
        prompt=prompt,
        max_tokens=100
    )
    return response['choices'][0]['text'].strip()

print(schedule_meeting("Can you schedule a meeting with John tomorrow at 3
PM?"))
```

Example 3: Restaurant Booking Chatbot

Scenario: A chatbot to book tables at a restaurant.

Implementation:

```
def restaurant_booking(user_input):
    prompt = f"""
    You are a restaurant booking assistant. The user wants to book a table.
Respond politely and ask for details.
    User: {user_input}
    """
    response = openai.Completion.create(
        model="text-davinci-003",
        prompt=prompt,
        max_tokens=150
    )
    return response['choices'][0]['text'].strip()

print(restaurant_booking("I need a table for 4 people this Friday at 7 PM."))
```

Challenges and Best Practices

- **Ambiguity**: Users may provide unclear inputs.
- **Error Handling**: Misunderstandings can disrupt the flow.
- **Scalability**: Supporting a high volume of interactions requires robust infrastructure.

Best Practices:

1. **Fallback Mechanisms**: Redirect users to human agents if the bot fails to resolve the issue.
2. **Continuous Training**: Regularly update the model with new conversation data.
3. **User Feedback**: Collect feedback to refine responses and improve user satisfaction.

Building conversational applications with LLMs is both an art and a science. By combining technical skills with user-centric design, you can create intelligent systems that deliver value and enhance user experiences. In the next chapter, we will explore how LLMs power search and recommendation engines, transforming how users discover information and content.

Chapter 6: Building Conversational Applications

Introduction:

Conversational applications, such as chatbots and virtual assistants, are among the most impactful use cases of large language models (LLMs). By leveraging the natural language understanding and generation capabilities of LLMs, developers can create applications that provide meaningful and context-aware interactions. This chapter will guide you through the process of designing and building conversational applications powered by LLMs.

Designing Conversational Interfaces

A successful conversational application starts with a well-thought-out design. This involves understanding user needs, defining the scope of the application, and crafting seamless interaction flows.

Key Considerations:

1. **User Intent Identification:**
   - Define the primary intents your application will address.
   - Categorize user queries into intents, such as "FAQ answering," "product support," or "recommendations."
2. **Conversational Flow:**
   - Map out how conversations will progress based on user inputs.
   - Incorporate fallback mechanisms for unrecognized inputs.
3. **Persona Development:**
   - Give your chatbot a personality that aligns with your brand or purpose.
   - For example, a financial assistant might adopt a professional and factual tone, while a virtual tutor could be more encouraging and conversational.

Example Conversation Flow:
```
User: "I need help with my order."
Bot: "Sure! Could you provide your order number?"
User: "It's 12345."
Bot: "Thank you. Let me check the details for order #12345."
```

Understanding Natural Language Understanding (NLU)

At the core of conversational applications is Natural Language Understanding (NLU), which allows the model to interpret user inputs. LLMs enhance NLU by providing contextual understanding and the ability to handle a wide range of inputs.

Steps in NLU:

1. **Intent Recognition:** Identify what the user wants based on their input.
2. **Entity Extraction:** Extract relevant details (e.g., dates, names, or order numbers).

3. **Context Retention:** Maintain context across multiple turns of a conversation to provide coherent responses.

Implementing Dialogue Management Systems

Dialogue management is the process of orchestrating conversations. It involves determining how the system responds to user inputs while maintaining context and guiding the conversation toward the intended goal.

Techniques for Dialogue Management:

1. **Rule-Based Systems:** Define explicit rules for conversation paths. These are simple but lack flexibility.
2. **State Machines:** Use a structured approach with defined states and transitions for managing dialogue.
3. **LLM-Based Approaches:** Leverage LLMs to dynamically generate responses based on the conversation history.

Example of State Transition:
```
State 1: Greet the user.
State 2: Ask for their query.
State 3: Provide a solution or escalate to support.
```

Enhancing Chatbot Performance with LLMs

While LLMs provide a strong foundation, optimizing their use for specific applications can significantly improve performance.

Techniques for Optimization:

1. **Context Windows:** Keep track of conversation history by feeding previous user inputs and bot responses as context. Example:
2. User: "Tell me about renewable energy."
3. Bot: "Renewable energy is derived from natural processes that are replenished constantly."
4. User: "Give me an example."
5. Bot: "Examples include solar energy and wind power."
6. **Few-Shot Learning:** Provide a few examples in the prompt to guide the model's responses. Example Prompt:
7. You are a helpful assistant. Respond to user queries with clear and concise answers.
8.
9. User: "What are the benefits of solar energy?"
10. Bot: "Solar energy is renewable, reduces electricity bills, and has low environmental impact."

11. User: "What are the drawbacks?"
12. **Error Handling and Fallbacks:** Anticipate potential errors and provide graceful fallbacks. Example:

13. Bot: "I'm sorry, I didn't catch that. Could you please rephrase?"
14. **Personalization:** Tailor responses to individual users by integrating user data and preferences.

Deployment and Maintenance

Deploying a conversational application requires ongoing monitoring and updates to ensure its effectiveness.

Steps for Deployment:

1. **Testing:** Conduct rigorous testing for diverse inputs and edge cases.
2. **Scaling:** Use cloud-based platforms to handle traffic spikes and ensure low-latency responses.
3. **Monitoring:** Track metrics such as user satisfaction, response accuracy, and latency.
4. **Iterative Improvement:** Continuously refine the bot based on user feedback and emerging requirements.

Building conversational applications with LLMs can unlock new levels of engagement and user satisfaction. The next chapter will explore how to develop intelligent search and recommendation systems, another transformative application of LLMs.

Chapter 7: Search and Recommendation Engines with LLMs

Introduction:

Search and recommendation engines play a critical role in enhancing user experience across various applications, from e-commerce platforms to content streaming services. Large language models (LLMs) bring unprecedented capabilities to these systems, enabling more accurate search results, personalized recommendations, and intuitive interactions. In this chapter, we will explore how to leverage LLMs to build advanced search and recommendation systems.

Role of LLMs in Search Optimization

Traditional search systems rely heavily on keyword matching and basic relevance algorithms. LLMs, on the other hand, excel at understanding the semantic meaning of queries and documents, allowing for more nuanced search results.

Key Advantages:

- **Semantic Understanding:** LLMs comprehend user intent beyond exact keyword matches.
- **Contextual Relevance:** They consider the broader context of a query to deliver accurate results.
- **Natural Language Processing (NLP):** Users can input queries in natural language without worrying about specific keywords.

Example: Imagine a user searching for "comfortable running shoes for marathons."

- **Traditional Search:** May prioritize pages containing exact matches for "running shoes" or "marathons."
- **LLM-Powered Search:** Understands the user's intent to find shoes designed for long-distance running and comfort, surfacing more relevant results.

Personalization with LLMs

LLMs enable highly personalized experiences by analyzing user behavior, preferences, and historical interactions. This capability is crucial for recommendation systems that aim to deliver tailored suggestions.

Implementation Steps:

1. **Data Collection:** Gather user interaction data such as clicks, views, and purchases.
2. **Embedding Generation:** Use LLMs to generate embeddings (numerical representations) for user profiles and items.
3. **Similarity Calculation:** Compare embeddings to find the closest matches.
4. **Feedback Loop:** Continuously refine recommendations based on user feedback.

Example: A movie streaming service can recommend films by analyzing:

- Past viewing history.
- Ratings provided by the user.
- Preferences of similar users.

Building Intelligent Recommendation Systems

Recommendation systems can leverage LLMs in various ways to enhance functionality and user satisfaction.

Collaborative Filtering:

- **How It Works:** Analyze patterns of user-item interactions.
- **LLM Role:** Generate embeddings for users and items, improving similarity calculations.

Content-Based Filtering:

- **How It Works:** Recommend items similar to those the user has engaged with.
- **LLM Role:** Understand item descriptions and user preferences at a deeper level.

Hybrid Systems:

- Combine collaborative and content-based filtering for optimal results.

Practical Example: An e-commerce platform uses an LLM-powered hybrid recommendation system:

- Suggests products similar to a user's previous purchases.
- Highlights trending items among users with similar profiles.

Case Studies of LLM-Enhanced Search and Recommendations

Case Study 1: E-Commerce Search Optimization

A leading online retailer implemented an LLM to enhance its search functionality. Results included:

- **Higher Conversion Rates:** Users found relevant products faster.
- **Improved Satisfaction:** Semantic understanding reduced irrelevant results.

Case Study 2: Personalized Content Streaming

A streaming service used LLMs to power recommendations, achieving:

- **Increased Engagement:** Users spent more time on the platform.

- **Better Retention:** Personalized suggestions matched user interests.

Tools and Frameworks for Implementation

Several tools can help in building search and recommendation systems with LLMs:

- **FAISS (Facebook AI Similarity Search):** Efficient similarity search and clustering of dense embeddings.
- **LangChain:** Facilitates the integration of LLMs for various applications, including search and recommendations.
- **ElasticSearch with LLMs:** Enhances traditional search engines with LLM capabilities.

Best Practices

1. **Focus on Relevance:** Ensure that search and recommendation outputs align closely with user intent.
2. **Optimize for Scalability:** Use efficient indexing and embedding storage techniques for large datasets.
3. **Incorporate User Feedback:** Continuously improve the system through explicit and implicit feedback.
4. **Prioritize Privacy:** Handle user data responsibly and comply with data protection regulations.

By integrating LLMs into search and recommendation engines, businesses can create intelligent, user-centric systems that deliver value and enhance user satisfaction. In the next chapter, we will explore how LLMs can bridge the gap between unstructured and structured data to unlock even more possibilities.

Chapter 8: Using LLMs with Structured Data

Introduction:

Large Language Models (LLMs) are predominantly designed to handle unstructured data, such as text, but they can also be leveraged to work with structured data, like databases, spreadsheets, and knowledge graphs. Integrating LLMs with structured data enables users to query, analyze, and interact with this data in more intuitive and natural ways. This chapter focuses on bridging the gap between unstructured and structured data, unlocking advanced use cases in data management and analysis.

Understanding Structured Data

Structured data is organized in a predefined schema, such as rows and columns in a database or fields in a JSON object. Common examples include:

- **Relational Databases**: SQL-based systems storing tabular data.
- **Spreadsheets**: Organized data in rows and columns.
- **Knowledge Graphs**: Representing entities and their relationships.
- **APIs**: Returning structured responses in formats like JSON or XML.

Despite its rigid format, structured data often contains metadata, descriptions, or fields that LLMs can process to provide insights.

Why Use LLMs with Structured Data?

1. Natural Language Queries

LLMs allow users to interact with structured data using natural language, eliminating the need for complex query languages like SQL.

- Example: Input: "Show me the top 5 best-selling products in the last quarter." Output: Results fetched and formatted from a sales database.

2. Contextual Insights

LLMs provide contextual insights by combining structured data with unstructured text, such as summarizing trends or anomalies.

Non-technical users can interact with complex datasets without learning specialized tools.

How LLMs Work with Structured Data

Step 1: Data Preprocessing

Data needs to be prepared before feeding it into an LLM:

1. **Extracting Relevant Data:** Identify the fields or rows relevant to the query.
2. **Formatting Data:** Convert structured data into a textual format.
   - Example:
   - Input JSON:
   - {
   -     "product": "Smartphone",
   -     "sales": 5000,
   -     "quarter": "Q1"
   - }

     Converted Text: "In Q1, the Smartphone had sales of 5000 units."

Step 2: Prompt Engineering

Crafting prompts to guide the LLM in processing structured data.

- Example Prompt:
- Analyze the following sales data and identify the top-performing product:
- Product: Smartphone, Sales: 5000
- Product: Laptop, Sales: 7000

  Product: Tablet, Sales: 3000

Step 3: Query Execution

Integrate the LLM with a database backend to fetch and manipulate data based on user queries.

- Example:
  - User Input: "Which region had the highest sales in Q2?"
  - Backend Process:
    1. Translate the query to SQL: `SELECT region, MAX(sales) FROM sales_data WHERE quarter='Q2';`
    2. Execute the query and format the response for the user.

Step 4: Post-Processing and Output

Enhance the raw data output by:

- Formatting results.
- Generating summaries or visualizations.
- Combining with unstructured insights.

Practical Examples

Example 1: Querying a Database

An HR department uses an LLM to query an employee database for headcount analysis.

1. **Prompt:**
2. Here is the employee data:
3. Department: Engineering, Employees: 50
4. Department: Marketing, Employees: 30
5. Department: Sales, Employees: 40
6.

   Question: Which department has the highest number of employees?

7. **LLM Response:** "The Engineering department has the highest number of employees with 50."
8. **SQL Translation (if backend integration is used):**

```
SELECT department, MAX(employees) FROM employee_data;
```

Example 2: Generating Insights from Financial Data

A financial analyst uses an LLM to identify trends from quarterly revenue reports.

1. **Input:**
2. Quarter: Q1, Revenue: $10M
3. Quarter: Q2, Revenue: $12M
4. Quarter: Q3, Revenue: $11M
5. Quarter: Q4, Revenue: $15M
6.

   Question: What is the revenue growth trend?

7. **LLM Response:** "Revenue shows a consistent upward trend, with the highest growth in Q4."
8. **Advanced Output:** Combine structured data with unstructured market analysis: "Q4 growth aligns with increased market demand due to seasonal promotions."

Example 3: Bridging Structured and Unstructured Data

A retail manager uses an LLM to analyze sales performance and customer feedback.

1. **Input:**
2. Sales Data:

```
3. Product: Headphones, Sales: 3000
4. Product: Speakers, Sales: 1500
5.
6. Feedback:
   "Customers appreciate the sound quality of the headphones but dislike
   the battery life."
```

7. **LLM Response:** "Headphones are performing well in sales, but addressing battery life issues could boost satisfaction and repeat purchases."

Advanced Use Cases

1. Knowledge Graph Integration

LLMs can interact with knowledge graphs to answer complex questions.

- Example: Query: "List all products linked to the 'Electronics' category with sales over 5000 units." Process:
  - Traverse the graph to find relevant nodes.
  - Use LLMs to summarize findings.

2. Automated Report Generation

LLMs can create detailed reports by combining structured data and unstructured insights.

- Example: Generate monthly sales reports with graphs, narratives, and actionable insights.

3. Conversational Interfaces

Integrate LLMs with structured data to power chatbots for:

- Customer service (e.g., order tracking).
- Employee support (e.g., querying HR policies).

Tools and Frameworks

1. LangChain

- Simplifies combining LLMs with databases and APIs.

2. OpenAI Functions

- Allows structured interaction with LLMs for natural language queries.

3. SQLAlchemy

- A Python toolkit for database integration.

4. Pandas and NumPy

- Useful for preprocessing and manipulating structured data before feeding it into LLMs.

Best Practices

1. **Optimize Data Formats:** Convert structured data into concise, readable text formats.
2. **Use Controlled Prompts:** Prevent ambiguous outputs by crafting specific prompts.
3. **Monitor Outputs:** Regularly evaluate LLM-generated responses for accuracy.
4. **Enhance Security:** Protect sensitive structured data using encryption and access controls.

Integrating LLMs with structured data opens up a new realm of possibilities, from simplified querying to intelligent analysis. By following the steps and examples in this chapter, you can unlock the potential of structured data in your applications, making it accessible and actionable for a wide range of users.

Chapter 9: Working with Code

Introduction:

Large Language Models (LLMs) have revolutionized the way developers approach software engineering tasks. From generating boilerplate code to debugging complex applications, LLMs bring efficiency, creativity, and precision to programming. This chapter delves into how LLMs are applied in coding workflows, along with best practices and real-world examples.

LLMs for Code Generation and Debugging

Code Generation

LLMs, like OpenAI Codex and GitHub Copilot, excel in generating code snippets, templates, and even entire functions based on natural language descriptions.

- **Example:** A developer inputs, "Write a Python function to calculate Fibonacci numbers," and the LLM generates a complete implementation.
- **Benefits:**
    o Saves time by reducing manual effort.
    o Helps developers unfamiliar with specific frameworks or languages.

Debugging

Identifying and resolving bugs is a crucial yet time-consuming task. LLMs assist in:

- **Code Analysis:** Reviewing code to identify potential errors or inefficiencies.
- **Error Explanation:** Providing detailed explanations of error messages and suggesting fixes.
- **Example:** For a Python error trace, the LLM can explain the issue and recommend modifications to resolve it.

Automating Software Development Tasks

LLMs enable automation in various stages of software development, streamlining processes and enhancing productivity.

Code Review Automation

- **Use Case:** Automatically reviewing pull requests to check for coding standard violations, potential bugs, or security vulnerabilities.
- **Example Tools:** ChatGPT integrated with CI/CD pipelines to flag issues in real-time.

- **Benefit:** Automates the creation of detailed and accurate documentation from code comments or function definitions.
- **Example:** Generating README files, API docs, or in-line comments based on existing code.

Test Case Generation

- **Use Case:** LLMs can generate unit tests, integration tests, or edge-case scenarios based on function descriptions or existing test suites.

Best Practices for Using LLMs in Programming

While LLMs offer remarkable capabilities, following best practices ensures their effective and responsible use:

1. **Understand Model Limitations:**
   - LLMs may occasionally generate incorrect or suboptimal code. Always verify outputs.
2. **Prompt Optimization:**
   - Write clear, concise prompts to improve the accuracy and relevance of the generated code.
3. **Iterative Feedback:**
   - Use an iterative approach to refine code generation or debugging suggestions.
4. **Integration with Existing Workflows:**
   - Seamlessly integrate LLMs with tools like IDEs, version control systems, and CI/CD pipelines.
5. **Prioritize Security:**
   - Ensure that LLMs do not inadvertently introduce vulnerabilities or expose sensitive data.

Examples of LLMs in Software Engineering

1. GitHub Copilot for Pair Programming

- Acts as a virtual pair programmer, offering real-time code suggestions based on the context.
- **Example:** While typing a React component, Copilot autocompletes props and state management logic.

2. Automating DevOps Tasks

- **Example:** Using an LLM to write infrastructure-as-code templates (e.g., Terraform scripts) based on high-level requirements.

- Developers paste code into ChatGPT and receive explanations for errors, along with suggestions to resolve them.

4. Codebase Exploration

- LLMs assist in understanding unfamiliar codebases by generating summaries or answering questions about specific functions or modules.

5. Learning and Skill Development

- **Example:** Junior developers use LLMs to quickly learn unfamiliar concepts, such as Kubernetes configurations or advanced SQL queries.

Complete Practical Example: Automating a Web Scraping Script

Scenario

A developer needs to create a web scraping script to extract product information (e.g., names, prices, and reviews) from an e-commerce website and save the data into a CSV file.

Step 1: Define Requirements

The developer provides the following prompt to the LLM:

"Write a Python script to scrape product names, prices, and reviews from an e-commerce website and save the data into a CSV file."

Step 2: LLM-Generated Code

The LLM generates the following script:

```
import requests
from bs4 import BeautifulSoup
import csv

# URL of the e-commerce website
url = "https://example.com/products"

# Send a GET request
response = requests.get(url)
soup = BeautifulSoup(response.content, "html.parser")

# Extract product details
products = []
for item in soup.find_all("div", class_="product-item"):
    name = item.find("h2", class_="product-name").text.strip()
    price = item.find("span", class_="price").text.strip()
```

```
    review = item.find("div", class_="review").text.strip()
    products.append([name, price, review])

# Save data to a CSV file
with open("products.csv", "w", newline="") as file:
    writer = csv.writer(file)
    writer.writerow(["Name", "Price", "Review"])
    writer.writerows(products)

print("Data saved to products.csv")
```

Step 3: Review and Validate the Code

The developer tests the script and finds it works as expected but decides to enhance error handling. They refine the prompt:

"Modify the script to include error handling for network issues and invalid HTML structure."

Step 4: Improved Script

The LLM generates an updated script:

```
import requests
from bs4 import BeautifulSoup
import csv

try:
    # URL of the e-commerce website
    url = "https://example.com/products"

    # Send a GET request
    response = requests.get(url, timeout=10)
    response.raise_for_status()
    soup = BeautifulSoup(response.content, "html.parser")

    # Extract product details
    products = []
    for item in soup.find_all("div", class_="product-item"):
        name = item.find("h2", class_="product-name")
        price = item.find("span", class_="price")
        review = item.find("div", class_="review")

        if name and price and review:
            products.append([name.text.strip(), price.text.strip(),
review.text.strip()])

    # Save data to a CSV file
    with open("products.csv", "w", newline="") as file:
        writer = csv.writer(file)
        writer.writerow(["Name", "Price", "Review"])
        writer.writerows(products)

    print("Data saved to products.csv")
```

```
except requests.exceptions.RequestException as e:
    print(f"Network error: {e}")
except Exception as e:
    print(f"An error occurred: {e}")
```

Step 5: Deploy and Monitor

The script is deployed as a scheduled task, and the developer uses the LLM to generate a monitoring script that sends email alerts if the scraping fails.

By iterating with an LLM, the developer efficiently creates a robust web scraping solution. This example demonstrates how LLMs can accelerate development while maintaining high-quality code.

Chapter 10: Building Multimodal Applications with LLMs

Combining Text, Image, and Video Data

Multimodal applications leverage diverse types of data such as text, images, and videos, enabling machines to perceive and process information similarly to humans. By combining these modalities, applications can:

- Enhance contextual understanding: Multimodal systems provide richer insights by correlating information from different sources.
- Enable complex use cases: For example, analyzing video content to generate captions or combining product images with descriptions for improved e-commerce search.
- Improve user experiences: Multimodal inputs create intuitive and natural interactions, like virtual assistants capable of understanding speech, recognizing gestures, and analyzing visual cues.

Challenges in Multimodal Integration

- **Data alignment**: Synchronizing and associating data from different modalities.
- **Processing complexities**: Handling the computational demands of multimodal data.
- **Model training**: Creating architectures that learn effectively from diverse data types.

Multimodal Model Capabilities

Modern LLMs and multimodal models, such as OpenAI's GPT-4 and DeepMind's Flamingo, exhibit remarkable capabilities in handling text, images, and videos together. Key features include:

1. Cross-Modal Understanding

- Recognizing relationships between text and visual elements (e.g., identifying objects in an image based on a textual query).
- Translating visual content into text and vice versa (e.g., caption generation or image synthesis).

2. Multi-Task Learning

- Models can perform various tasks simultaneously, such as:
  - Object detection in images.
  - Sentiment analysis of captions.

o   Generating video descriptions.

3. Natural Interactions

- Understanding speech, gestures, and images for immersive applications such as augmented reality and gaming.

4. Few-Shot and Zero-Shot Learning

- Adapting to new tasks with minimal data by leveraging pre-trained knowledge.

Applications of Multimodal LLMs

1. Content Creation

- Generating rich multimedia content such as videos with captions, infographics, and interactive presentations.

2. Healthcare

- Analyzing X-rays or MRIs while processing patient reports for diagnosis.
- Assisting in surgery with real-time image and data analysis.

3. E-Commerce

- Enhancing product discovery by combining image recognition with natural language search (e.g., "Find shirts similar to this image").
- Personalized recommendations based on user preferences in text and visual formats.

4. Education

- Creating interactive learning materials that combine text, visuals, and videos for enhanced comprehension.

5. Autonomous Systems

- Enabling self-driving cars to interpret visual road signs and audio commands simultaneously.
- Facilitating robots that interact with humans and environments naturally.

6. Entertainment

- Powering virtual influencers or characters capable of conversing, expressing emotions, and generating multimedia content.

Tools and Frameworks for Multimodal Development

Several tools and frameworks simplify the development of multimodal applications:

1. Transformers Library by Hugging Face

- Supports multimodal models like DALL-E, CLIP, and Flamingo.
- Provides pre-trained models and utilities for customization.

2. OpenAI API

- Offers GPT models with multimodal capabilities for text and image understanding.

3. TensorFlow and PyTorch

- Popular deep learning frameworks for developing custom multimodal architectures.
- Includes tools for handling text, image, and video datasets.

4. Microsoft's MMF (Multimodal Framework)

- A unified framework for training and evaluating multimodal models.
- Simplifies dataset preparation and evaluation.

5. OpenCV

- Facilitates image and video processing.
- Useful for pre-processing visual data before integration with models.

6. Speech-to-Text and Text-to-Speech APIs

- Convert speech to text and vice versa for audio-visual applications.
- Examples: Google Speech-to-Text, Amazon Polly.

By integrating text, image, and video data, multimodal applications can deliver unparalleled functionality and user experiences. The next sections will explore fine-tuning techniques to customize these capabilities for specific needs.

Chapter 11: Fine-Tuning Large Language Models

Introduction:

Fine-tuning is a crucial process in customizing large language models (LLMs) to perform specific tasks or align them with particular domains. In this chapter, we will explore the techniques, tools, and best practices for fine-tuning LLMs, offering both theoretical insights and practical guidance.

Overview of Fine-Tuning Techniques

Fine-tuning is the process of taking a pre-trained LLM and adapting it to a specialized dataset. This involves training the model on domain-specific data while retaining its general language capabilities. Key techniques include:

1. **Standard Fine-Tuning**:
   o   Involves training the entire model on a labeled dataset.
   o   Suitable for tasks requiring domain-specific knowledge.
2. **Parameter-Efficient Fine-Tuning**:
   o   Techniques such as LoRA (Low-Rank Adaptation) or Adapter Layers modify only a subset of model parameters.
   o   Reduces computational costs and memory requirements.
3. **Prompt-Based Fine-Tuning**:
   o   Adjusts the model's behavior by designing task-specific prompts.
   o   Avoids modifying the model parameters.
4. **Instruction Fine-Tuning**:
   o   Trains the model to follow specific instructions or adhere to particular styles.
   o   Commonly used for improving conversational capabilities.

Dataset Preparation for Fine-Tuning

A well-prepared dataset is the foundation of successful fine-tuning. Follow these steps to ensure data quality and relevance:

1. Data Collection:

- Identify sources of domain-specific text, such as research papers, user logs, or product descriptions.
- Ensure diversity to cover different scenarios.

2. Data Cleaning:

- Remove duplicates, irrelevant content, and inconsistencies.

- Normalize text for uniform formatting.

3. Data Annotation:

- Label datasets with appropriate task-specific tags (e.g., sentiment labels, named entities).
- Use tools like Prodigy or Label Studio for annotation.

4. Data Splitting:

- Split data into training, validation, and test sets (e.g., 80/10/10 split).
- Maintain class balance to prevent bias.

Practical Example: Dataset for Customer Support

Suppose you're fine-tuning an LLM for a customer support chatbot. Your dataset might include:

- **Training Data**: Historical chat logs with labeled intents (e.g., "Billing Inquiry", "Technical Issue").
- **Validation Data**: Recently collected conversations to test performance during training.
- **Test Data**: Held-out data to evaluate the final model.

Best Practices for Model Customization

Fine-tuning LLMs can be resource-intensive, so optimizing the process is essential:

1. **Start Small**:
   o Fine-tune smaller versions of the model to validate feasibility before scaling up.
2. **Use Pretrained Checkpoints**:
   o Begin with checkpoints optimized for related tasks to reduce training time.
3. **Optimize Hyperparameters**:
   o Experiment with learning rates, batch sizes, and epochs to achieve optimal performance.
4. **Monitor Overfitting**:
   o Use validation metrics to ensure the model generalizes well to unseen data.
5. **Leverage Transfer Learning**:
   o Use fine-tuned models as baselines for similar tasks to reduce redundancy.

Evaluating and Testing Fine-Tuned Models

Evaluation is critical to assess the performance and reliability of the fine-tuned model:

1. Quantitative Metrics:

- **Accuracy**: Percentage of correct predictions.
- **Precision, Recall, F1-Score**: Evaluate performance for classification tasks.
- **BLEU/ROUGE Scores**: Measure quality of text generation.

2. Qualitative Analysis:

- Review model outputs for coherence, relevance, and fluency.
- Perform error analysis to identify common failure points.

3. A/B Testing:

- Compare the fine-tuned model with existing solutions to measure improvements.

Practical Example: Testing a Sentiment Analysis Model

After fine-tuning an LLM for sentiment analysis on customer reviews:

- **Metrics**: Achieve an F1-Score of 92% on the test set.
- **Sample Analysis**: Ensure correct classification of ambiguous reviews (e.g., "The product is great, but delivery was slow.").

By mastering fine-tuning, you can unlock the true potential of LLMs, adapting them to meet specific needs and driving impactful outcomes. The next chapter will explore responsible AI practices, emphasizing the ethical considerations of using LLMs.

Chapter 12: Responsible AI

Introduction:

As Large Language Models (LLMs) become integral to applications across industries, it is essential to ensure their deployment aligns with ethical principles and societal values. This chapter delves into the key aspects of responsible AI, focusing on addressing biases, ensuring privacy, and complying with regulations.

Ethical Considerations for Using LLMs

LLMs are powerful tools, but their impact on users and society must be carefully managed. Key ethical considerations include:

1. **Bias and Fairness**:
   - LLMs may reflect biases present in their training data, leading to unfair outcomes.
   - Mitigation strategies:
     - Use diverse and balanced training datasets.
     - Apply fairness-aware algorithms during fine-tuning.
2. **Transparency**:
   - Users should understand how the model generates outputs.
   - Provide explainability mechanisms to clarify decisions or predictions.
3. **Accountability**:
   - Developers and organizations must take responsibility for the model's behavior.
   - Establish clear guidelines for addressing harmful outputs.

Addressing Bias and Fairness

Bias in LLMs can perpetuate stereotypes and lead to discrimination. Steps to address this include:

1. **Dataset Audits**:
   - Regularly review training data for representation gaps and biases.
   - Example: Analyze sentiment distributions across different demographic groups.
2. **Bias Testing**:
   - Evaluate model outputs for unintended biases using test cases or benchmarks.
   - Example: Use tools like Microsoft's Fairlearn to identify and mitigate disparities.
3. **Continuous Monitoring**:
   - Track model performance in real-world settings to identify emerging biases.

Ensuring Privacy and Security

Data privacy and security are paramount when deploying LLMs, particularly in sensitive applications.

1. **Data Anonymization**:
   - Remove personally identifiable information (PII) from training and input data.
2. **Secure Storage**:
   - Encrypt training datasets and model checkpoints.
3. **Minimizing Data Retention**:
   - Avoid storing user inputs unless necessary for performance improvement.
4. **Adversarial Testing**:
   - Simulate attacks to identify vulnerabilities and enhance model robustness.

Regulatory Compliance and LLMs

Adhering to laws and regulations is critical for responsible AI deployment. Key areas include:

1. **Data Protection Regulations**:
   - Ensure compliance with laws such as GDPR (General Data Protection Regulation) and CCPA (California Consumer Privacy Act).
   - Example: Provide users with opt-in and opt-out options for data usage.
2. **Content Moderation Laws**:
   - Implement safeguards to prevent the generation of harmful or illegal content.
3. **AI Governance Frameworks**:
   - Align with industry standards and best practices, such as those outlined by the OECD or ISO.

Case Study: Responsible AI in Healthcare Chatbots

Scenario:

A healthcare provider deploys an LLM-powered chatbot to assist patients with medical inquiries.

Challenges:

1. **Bias**: The chatbot's advice might favor certain demographics due to skewed training data.
2. **Privacy**: Patient data must remain confidential.
3. **Compliance**: The system must adhere to HIPAA regulations.

Solutions:

1. **Bias Mitigation**:
   o Fine-tune the chatbot using diverse medical datasets.
2. **Privacy Safeguards**:
   o Encrypt patient interactions and anonymize records.
3. **Compliance Measures**:
   o Regular audits to ensure adherence to HIPAA and other standards.

Chapter 13: Emerging Trends and Innovations

Introduction:

The field of Large Language Models (LLMs) is rapidly evolving, driven by breakthroughs in AI research and new applications across industries. This chapter explores emerging trends and innovations shaping the future of LLMs.

1. Scaling LLM Architectures

The trend of building larger and more capable LLMs continues to dominate the field. Key aspects include:

1. **Parameter Growth**:
   - Models are expanding from billions to trillions of parameters, enabling them to capture more nuanced knowledge.
   - Example: Models like GPT-4 and beyond demonstrate unprecedented understanding and generation capabilities.
2. **Efficient Scaling**:
   - Innovations such as sparse architectures and mixture-of-experts reduce computational overhead while maintaining performance.

2. Multimodal Capabilities

The integration of text, image, and video processing is unlocking new possibilities for LLMs.

1. **Unified Models**:
   - Multimodal LLMs like OpenAI's DALL-E and DeepMind's Flamingo can process and generate diverse data types.
2. **Applications**:
   - Enhanced virtual assistants capable of understanding and generating multimedia content.
   - Example: AI-powered tools for graphic design that combine textual input with image generation.

3. Real-Time Adaptation

LLMs are evolving to adapt in real-time to changing user requirements and environments.

1. **On-the-Fly Fine-Tuning**:
   o Techniques like low-latency adapters enable models to be fine-tuned during deployment.
2. **Personalization**:
   o Real-time learning from user feedback allows models to deliver more tailored outputs.

---

4. Enhanced Explainability

Improving the interpretability of LLMs is a key research area, particularly for high-stakes applications.

1. **Attention Mechanisms**:
   o Visualization tools highlight how models focus on input data when generating outputs.
2. **Post-Hoc Analysis**:
   o Techniques like LIME and SHAP provide insights into decision-making processes.

---

5. Responsible AI Innovations

The focus on ethical and transparent AI development continues to grow.

1. **Bias Mitigation Tools**:
   o Frameworks for detecting and addressing biases in training data and model outputs.
2. **Regulation Compliance**:
   o Automated tools ensure models adhere to global and local AI regulations.

---

6. Quantum Computing and LLMs

Quantum computing promises to revolutionize LLM training and deployment.

1. **Accelerated Training**:
   o Quantum algorithms can significantly speed up matrix operations used in training.
2. **New Architectures**:
   o Quantum-inspired neural networks may unlock new capabilities.

---

7. Democratization of LLMs

Efforts to make LLMs accessible to a broader audience are gaining momentum.

1. **Open-Source Models**:
   o Projects like Hugging Face's Transformers provide easy access to state-of-the-art models.
2. **Low-Cost Deployment**:
   o Optimized inference techniques reduce resource requirements for running LLMs.

Case Study: Future of Education with LLMs

Scenario:

An educational platform integrates LLMs to enhance personalized learning.

Innovations:

1. **Adaptive Learning**:
   o Models adjust content difficulty based on student performance.
2. **Interactive Tutorials**:
   o Multimodal LLMs combine video, text, and quizzes for immersive experiences.

Impact:

1. Improved engagement and knowledge retention.
2. Access to high-quality education for underserved communities.

As the field advances, staying updated with these trends will be crucial for leveraging LLMs effectively. This concludes our exploration of Large Language Models and their transformative potential across industries.

Part –II: Let us implement LLM Model

Large Language Models (LLMs) enable the creation of a wide range of intelligent applications and agents that leverage their natural language understanding and generation capabilities. Here are some examples:

Part –II: Implementation of LLM Model

Outlines:

14. Conversational Agents and Chatbots

- **Customer Support Bots:** Handle customer inquiries, complaints, and FAQs.
- **Virtual Assistants:** Perform tasks like setting reminders, scheduling, or answering general questions (e.g., Siri, Alexa).
- **Therapy Bots:** Provide mental health support and basic counseling (e.g., Woebot).

15. Content Generation Applications

- **Article and Blog Writing Tools:** Generate content drafts for blogs, articles, and other publications.
- **Creative Writing Apps:** Assist in writing poetry, novels, or scripts.
- **Social Media Content Creators:** Generate captions, posts, and engagement content for platforms.

16. Personalized Learning Platforms

- **Tutoring Systems:** Explain concepts, answer student questions, or help with homework.
- **Language Learning Apps:** Offer conversational practice and personalized feedback.
- **Exam Preparation Tools:** Create quizzes, flashcards, and summaries of study material.

17. Code Generation and Debugging Tools

- **Code Assistants:** Generate, explain, and debug code snippets (e.g., GitHub Copilot).
- **API Documentation Tools:** Automate the creation of technical documentation.
- **Code Review Tools:** Analyze codebases for errors or inefficiencies.

18. Search and Recommendation Systems

- **Semantic Search Engines:** Provide context-aware search results.
- **Recommendation Engines:** Offer product, movie, or book recommendations based on user preferences.
- **Knowledge Bases:** Summarize and retrieve relevant information from large datasets.

19. Intelligent Writing Assistants

- **Grammar and Style Checkers:** Offer corrections and suggestions to improve writing (e.g., Grammarly).
- **Summarization Tools:** Condense articles, reports, or books into concise summaries.
- **Personalized Email Assistants:** Draft and reply to emails effectively.

20. Healthcare Applications

- **Medical Query Assistants:** Answer patient queries and provide preliminary medical advice.
- **Symptom Checkers:** Analyze symptoms and provide potential diagnoses.
- **Document Processing:** Extract and summarize data from clinical notes and research papers.

21. E-Commerce and Retail

- **Virtual Shopping Assistants:** Guide users through product searches and purchases.
- **Personalized Product Descriptions:** Automatically generate descriptions tailored to a target audience.
- **Review Analysis Tools:** Summarize or analyze customer reviews for insights.

22. Legal and Financial Assistants

- **Legal Document Summarizers:** Extract key points from lengthy contracts and legal texts.
- **Tax Assistants:** Help users understand tax filing requirements.
- **Investment Advisors:** Provide financial insights and portfolio recommendations.

23. Multimodal Applications

- **Image-to-Text Generators:** Describe images or analyze visual content.
- **Video Summarizers:** Generate summaries of video content.
- **Speech-to-Text and Text-to-Speech Integrations:** Combine voice and text capabilities for accessibility or entertainment.

24. Enterprise Tools

- **Employee Training Systems:** Customize onboarding materials and training content.
- **Meeting Assistants:** Summarize meeting notes and action items.
- **HR Tools:** Assist with job descriptions, recruitment, and employee feedback analysis.

25. Gaming and Entertainment

- **Dynamic NPCs (Non-Player Characters):** Create interactive, realistic dialogues for video games.
- **Story Generators:** Build immersive narratives based on user input.
- **Game Assistants:** Help players with hints, walkthroughs, or strategy tips.

26. Research and Scientific Applications

- **Paper Reviewers:** Summarize or critique research papers.
- **Data Insights Tools:** Assist with interpreting and visualizing complex datasets.
- **Idea Generators:** Support brainstorming for new research avenues.

27. Accessibility Solutions

- **Assistive Technologies:** Help users with disabilities by providing speech-to-text, text-to-speech, or simplified content.
- **Language Translation Tools:** Provide real-time translation in various languages.
- **Reading Aids:** Summarize or explain complex content in simpler terms.

28. Creative Applications

- **Music and Lyric Generators:** Create original music compositions or song lyrics.
- **Art Descriptions:** Generate captions or context for visual art.
- **Interactive Storytelling:** Allow users to co-create stories by engaging with an LLM.

29. Responsible AI Solutions

- **Content Moderation Tools:** Detect and filter harmful, offensive, or inappropriate content.
- **Bias Detection Tools:** Analyze content for potential bias or harmful stereotypes.
- **Ethics Advisors:** Provide recommendations on ethical considerations in AI applications.

---

30. Emerging Use Cases

- **Autonomous Agents:** Develop self-guiding systems for specific tasks (e.g., AutoGPT).
- **Dynamic Marketing Campaigns:** Create personalized advertisements and content strategies.
- **Virtual Companions:** Provide company and emotional support to users.

Chapter No. 14 Conversational Agents and Chatbots

Customer Support Bot:

Let's start developing a **Customer Support Bot**. We'll break the process into manageable steps, so you can follow along easily. The bot will handle customer inquiries, complaints, and FAQs effectively using a combination of a conversational framework and an LLM like OpenAI's GPT models.

Step 1: Define the Scope

Decide the functionality and features of your bot:

- **Answer FAQs**: Provide quick responses to frequent questions.
- **Complaint Logging**: Capture user complaints and store them.
- **Inquiry Handling**: Answer generic and product/service-specific queries.
- **Escalation**: Notify human agents when necessary.
- **Language Support**: Decide on supported languages.
- **Platform**: Web, mobile app, social media (e.g., WhatsApp, Messenger).

Step 2: Choose Technology Stack

- **Frontend**:
    - Web: HTML, CSS, JavaScript (React/Angular/Vue.js)
    - Chat widget: Tawk.to, Intercom
- **Backend**:
    - Python (Flask/Django/FastAPI) or Node.js
- **LLM API**: OpenAI (GPT-4) or similar.
- **Database**: MongoDB, PostgreSQL, or Firebase for storing conversations and complaints.
- **Integration Tools**: Twilio, Slack, or WhatsApp APIs.

Step 3: Design the Bot's Flow

- **Greeting**: Welcome users and ask how you can help.
- **Intent Recognition**: Detect the user's intent using keywords or an LLM.
- **Response Generation**:
    - Direct response for FAQs.
    - Logging mechanism for complaints.
    - Information retrieval for inquiries.
- **Fallback and Escalation**: Handle unrecognized inputs gracefully and pass to a human agent.

Step 4: Implement Core Code

Here's a basic Python example using **Flask** and OpenAI's API for conversational logic.

1. Setup Environment

Install dependencies:

```
pip install flask openai
```

2. Basic Bot Code

```python
Copy code
from flask import Flask, request, jsonify
import openai

# Initialize Flask app
app = Flask(__name__)

# OpenAI API Key
openai.api_key = "your_openai_api_key"

# Sample FAQs
FAQS = {
    "What is your return policy?": "You can return any item within 30 days of purchase.",
    "How can I track my order?": "You can track your order using the tracking link sent to your email.",
    "What are your customer service hours?": "Our customer service is available 24/7."
}

@app.route("/chat", methods=["POST"])
def chat():
    user_input = request.json.get("message", "")

    # Check FAQs first
    if user_input in FAQS:
        return jsonify({"response": FAQS[user_input]})

    # Use LLM for more complex responses
    response = openai.Completion.create(
        engine="text-davinci-003",
        prompt=f"You are a helpful customer support bot. Answer: {user_input}",
        max_tokens=150
    )
    return jsonify({"response": response.choices[0].text.strip()})

if __name__ == "__main__":
    app.run(debug=True)
```

Step 5: Add Logging for Complaints

Modify the bot to log complaints in a database:

```python
```

```
Copy code
import sqlite3

# Connect to SQLite database
def log_complaint(user_input):
    conn = sqlite3.connect('complaints.db')
    cursor = conn.cursor()
    cursor.execute("""
        CREATE TABLE IF NOT EXISTS complaints (
            id INTEGER PRIMARY KEY AUTOINCREMENT,
            complaint TEXT
        )
    """)
    cursor.execute("INSERT INTO complaints (complaint) VALUES (?)",
(user_input,))
    conn.commit()
    conn.close()

@app.route("/chat", methods=["POST"])
def chat():
    user_input = request.json.get("message", "")

    # Check for complaint keyword
    if "complaint" in user_input.lower():
        log_complaint(user_input)
        return jsonify({"response": "Your complaint has been logged. We will
get back to you shortly."})

    # Handle FAQs and other queries as before
```

Step 6: Test and Iterate

- **Test Scenarios**: Simulate various customer queries.
- **Improve Responses**: Adjust prompts and FAQ mappings based on feedback.
- **Add Features**: Include multi-turn conversations, sentiment analysis, or integration with ticketing systems like Zendesk.

Step 7: Deploy

Deploy your bot on a platform:

- **Local Server**: Use Flask's built-in server for testing.
- **Cloud Deployment**: Use AWS, Heroku, or Azure for production.
- **Integrate Chat Interface**: Add a chat widget to your website or app.

1. Virtual Assistant

Let's start developing a **Virtual Assistant** that involves integrating functionalities like reminders, scheduling, and answering general questions. Here's how we can build one step by step using **Python**, an **LLM API**, and optional third-party services (e.g., Google Calendar API).

Step 1: Define Features

Your virtual assistant should:

1. **Set Reminders**: Let users set timed reminders.
2. **Schedule Events**: Allow integration with a calendar to schedule events.
3. **Answer General Questions**: Use an LLM for Q&A capabilities.
4. **Perform Simple Tasks**: Provide weather updates, math calculations, or play music (optional).

Step 2: Choose Technology Stack

- **Programming Language**: Python
- **LLM API**: OpenAI API (GPT-4) or similar.
- **Calendar Integration**: Google Calendar API or Outlook Calendar.
- **Voice Interface**: SpeechRecognition (optional).
- **Frontend (Optional)**: Use a chatbot UI or voice interface.

Step 3: Set Up Environment

Install required libraries:

```bash
Copy code
pip install flask openai google-auth google-auth-oauthlib google-auth-
httplib2 google-api-python-client schedule
```

Step 4: Implement Core Code

Here's an example implementation for a virtual assistant with reminders, scheduling, and general Q&A.

1. Base Flask App

Create the app with endpoints for user interaction.

```python
python
Copy code
from flask import Flask, request, jsonify
import openai
import datetime
import schedule
import time
from threading import Thread

# Initialize Flask app
app = Flask(__name__)

# OpenAI API Key
openai.api_key = "your_openai_api_key"

# In-memory storage for reminders
reminders = []

# General Questions using GPT
@app.route("/ask", methods=["POST"])
def ask():
    user_question = request.json.get("question", "")
    response = openai.Completion.create(
        engine="text-davinci-003",
        prompt=f"You are a helpful virtual assistant. Answer the following: {user_question}",
        max_tokens=150
    )
    return jsonify({"answer": response.choices[0].text.strip()})

# Add Reminder
@app.route("/reminder", methods=["POST"])
def set_reminder():
    data = request.json
    time_str = data.get("time")
    message = data.get("message")

    reminder_time = datetime.datetime.strptime(time_str, "%Y-%m-%d %H:%M:%S")
    reminders.append({"time": reminder_time, "message": message})
    return jsonify({"status": "Reminder set successfully!"})

# Check Reminders
def check_reminders():
    while True:
        now = datetime.datetime.now()
        for reminder in reminders[:]:
            if now >= reminder["time"]:
                print(f"Reminder: {reminder['message']}")
                reminders.remove(reminder)
        time.sleep(1)

# Start Flask server and reminder thread
if __name__ == "__main__":
    Thread(target=check_reminders, daemon=True).start()
    app.run(debug=True)
```

2. Integrate Calendar (Optional)

Integrate Google Calendar API for scheduling.

Set up Google Calendar API:

1. Go to Google Cloud Console.
2. Create a project and enable the **Google Calendar API**.
3. Download the credentials JSON file.

Code for Calendar Integration:

```python
Copy code
from google.oauth2.credentials import Credentials
from googleapiclient.discovery import build

# Google Calendar Integration
def create_event(summary, start_time, end_time):
    creds = Credentials.from_authorized_user_file('credentials.json',
['https://www.googleapis.com/auth/calendar'])
    service = build('calendar', 'v3', credentials=creds)

    event = {
        'summary': summary,
        'start': {'dateTime': start_time, 'timeZone': 'UTC'},
        'end': {'dateTime': end_time, 'timeZone': 'UTC'}
    }
    event = service.events().insert(calendarId='primary',
body=event).execute()
    return f"Event created: {event['htmlLink']}"

@app.route("/schedule", methods=["POST"])
def schedule_event():
    data = request.json
    summary = data.get("summary")
    start_time = data.get("start_time")
    end_time = data.get("end_time")

    event_link = create_event(summary, start_time, end_time)
    return jsonify({"status": "Event scheduled!", "link": event_link})
```

Step 5: Add Voice Interface (Optional)

Use `SpeechRecognition` and `pyttsx3` for speech-to-text and text-to-speech capabilities:

```python
Copy code
import pyttsx3
import speech_recognition as sr
```

```python
# Initialize text-to-speech
engine = pyttsx3.init()

def speak(text):
    engine.say(text)
    engine.runAndWait()

# Speech-to-text
def listen():
    recognizer = sr.Recognizer()
    with sr.Microphone() as source:
        print("Listening...")
        audio = recognizer.listen(source)
        try:
            return recognizer.recognize_google(audio)
        except sr.UnknownValueError:
            return "Sorry, I didn't catch that."

# Example interaction
while True:
    user_input = listen()
    if "reminder" in user_input.lower():
        speak("What reminder would you like to set?")
        reminder = listen()
        speak(f"Setting a reminder for: {reminder}")
    elif "stop" in user_input.lower():
        speak("Goodbye!")
        break
```

Step 6: Deploy

- **Deploy Locally**: Run the app on `localhost`.
- **Cloud Deployment**: Use AWS, Azure, or Heroku for a scalable solution.
- **Integration**: Embed the assistant in web or mobile apps, or use it on platforms like WhatsApp or Telegram via their APIs.

Future Enhancements

- **Weather Updates**: Integrate a weather API.
- **Music Playback**: Use Spotify API for music.
- **IoT Integration**: Connect to smart home devices.
- **Multilingual Support**: Enable interactions in multiple languages.

2. Therapy Bot:

Therapy Bot is a meaningful project that requires thoughtful design to ensure user well-being, ethical considerations, and privacy protection. Such bots can offer **emotional support, stress management techniques, and guided self-help exercises**, but they must also include clear disclaimers that they are not substitutes for professional therapy.

Step 1: Define Features

Core features for a therapy bot:

1. **Mood Tracking**: Ask users how they feel and track changes over time.
2. **Guided Exercises**: Offer mindfulness, breathing exercises, or gratitude journaling.
3. **CBT Techniques**: Provide Cognitive Behavioral Therapy-style responses (e.g., reframing negative thoughts).
4. **General Chat**: Listen to users and provide supportive, empathetic responses.
5. **Emergency Guidance**: Direct users to crisis resources if they mention harmful thoughts.
6. **Privacy and Security**: Ensure user data is encrypted and not stored without consent.

Step 2: Choose Technology Stack

- **Frontend**: Web app (React, Angular) or mobile app (Flutter, React Native).
- **Backend**: Python (Flask, Django) or Node.js.
- **LLM API**: OpenAI API (GPT-4) or similar.
- **Database**: Firebase, MongoDB, or PostgreSQL.
- **Deployment**: AWS, Heroku, or Azure.

Step 3: Implement Core Bot Functionality

1. Set Up Environment

Install required libraries:

```bash
Copy code
pip install flask openai
```

2. Basic Therapy Bot Code

Here's a starting point for your therapy bot.

```python
```

```
Copy code
from flask import Flask, request, jsonify
import openai
import datetime

# Initialize Flask app
app = Flask(__name__)

# OpenAI API Key
openai.api_key = "your_openai_api_key"

# Mood tracking storage (in-memory for simplicity)
user_moods = []

@app.route("/mood", methods=["POST"])
def mood_check():
    """Track and respond to user mood."""
    mood = request.json.get("mood", "").lower()
    timestamp = datetime.datetime.now()

    # Store mood
    user_moods.append({"mood": mood, "timestamp": timestamp})

    # Respond to mood
    if mood in ["sad", "anxious", "stressed"]:
        response = "I'm sorry you're feeling this way. Would you like to try
a mindfulness exercise?"
    elif mood in ["happy", "content", "relaxed"]:
        response = "That's wonderful! Keep focusing on what brings you joy."
    else:
        response = "Thank you for sharing. Remember, I'm here to help
whenever you need."

    return jsonify({"response": response})

@app.route("/chat", methods=["POST"])
def therapy_chat():
    """Provide empathetic chat responses using LLM."""
    user_message = request.json.get("message", "")

    response = openai.Completion.create(
        engine="text-davinci-003",
        prompt=f"You are a supportive therapy bot. Respond empathetically and
helpfully to: {user_message}",
        max_tokens=150
    )
    return jsonify({"response": response.choices[0].text.strip()})

@app.route("/exercise", methods=["GET"])
def mindfulness_exercise():
    """Provide a mindfulness exercise."""
    exercises = [
        "Take a deep breath in for 4 seconds, hold for 7 seconds, and exhale
slowly for 8 seconds. Repeat this three times.",
        "Write down three things you are grateful for today.",
        "Take a moment to focus on your surroundings. Notice three things you
can see, hear, and feel.",
```

```
    ]
    return jsonify({"exercise": exercises})

if __name__ == "__main__":
    app.run(debug=True)
```

Step 4: Add Advanced Features

1. Mood Analysis and Sentiment Tracking

Use an LLM to analyze user input and classify mood dynamically:

```python
Copy code
@app.route("/analyze_mood", methods=["POST"])
def analyze_mood():
    user_message = request.json.get("message", "")
    response = openai.Completion.create(
        engine="text-davinci-003",
        prompt=f"Analyze the mood of the following message: {user_message}",
        max_tokens=50
    )
    mood = response.choices[0].text.strip()
    return jsonify({"mood": mood})
```

2. Crisis Intervention

Redirect users in crisis to appropriate resources:

```python
Copy code
@app.route("/emergency", methods=["POST"])
def emergency():
    user_message = request.json.get("message", "")

    if "harm" in user_message.lower() or "suicide" in user_message.lower():
        response = "I'm sorry you're feeling this way. Please reach out to a
professional or contact a crisis hotline like 988 (in the U.S.)."
    else:
        response = "I'm here to listen and help. Tell me more about how
you're feeling."

    return jsonify({"response": response})
```

3. Journaling

Let users write daily journals and retrieve them:

```python
Copy code
journals = []
```

```
@app.route("/journal", methods=["POST"])
def add_journal():
    entry = request.json.get("entry", "")
    timestamp = datetime.datetime.now()
    journals.append({"entry": entry, "timestamp": timestamp})
    return jsonify({"response": "Your journal entry has been saved."})

@app.route("/journal", methods=["GET"])
def get_journals():
    return jsonify({"journals": journals})
```

Step 5: Privacy and Security

- **Data Encryption**: Use HTTPS for all data transmissions.
- **Storage Security**: Encrypt user data in databases.
- **Anonymity**: Avoid storing identifiable user information unless explicitly agreed.

Step 6: Deploy

1. Test the bot locally.
2. Deploy on a platform like AWS, Heroku, or Azure.
3. Optionally, integrate the bot with platforms like WhatsApp, Messenger, or Telegram.

Step 7: Add Disclaimer

Include a clear disclaimer:

- The bot is not a substitute for professional help.
- Users in crisis should contact a licensed therapist or a crisis hotline.

Step 8: Future Enhancements

- **Multilingual Support**: Use translation APIs to handle different languages.
- **Behavioral Insights**: Offer insights based on user interactions over time.
- **Gamification**: Add rewards or achievements for completing exercises.

Chapter 15: Content Generation

Introduction:

Content Generation Application powered by an **LLM (Large Language Model)** can help users generate articles, blogs, product descriptions, social media posts, or any other type of content. Here's how to build such an application step by step.

Step 1: Define the Features

Your content generation app can include:

1. **Text Generation**: Create custom content based on user prompts.
2. **Tone and Style Customization**: Allow users to specify tone (formal, casual, humorous, etc.) and style (persuasive, descriptive, etc.).
3. **Content Templates**: Provide pre-defined templates for blogs, emails, ads, or product descriptions.
4. **Keyword Optimization**: Help users incorporate specific keywords for SEO.
5. **Multilingual Support**: Generate content in different languages.
6. **Plagiarism Detection**: Ensure generated content is unique (optional integration).

Step 2: Choose the Technology Stack

- **Frontend**: React, Angular, or Vue.js for web apps; Flutter or React Native for mobile apps.
- **Backend**: Python (Flask, FastAPI, or Django).
- **LLM API**: OpenAI API (GPT-4), Anthropic Claude, or similar.
- **Database**: Firebase, MongoDB, or PostgreSQL for storing templates, user preferences, and generated content.
- **Deployment**: AWS, Heroku, or Azure.

Step 3: Set Up the Development Environment

Install required libraries:

```bash
Copy code
pip install flask openai langdetect
```

Step 4: Basic Application Code

Here's a basic Flask backend for the content generation app.

1. Flask Backend

```python
Copy code
from flask import Flask, request, jsonify
import openai
from langdetect import detect

# Initialize Flask app
app = Flask(__name__)

# OpenAI API Key
openai.api_key = "your_openai_api_key"

@app.route("/generate", methods=["POST"])
def generate_content():
    """Generate content based on user input."""
    data = request.json
    prompt = data.get("prompt", "")
    tone = data.get("tone", "neutral")
    style = data.get("style", "descriptive")
    language = data.get("language", "en")  # Default to English

    # LLM Prompt Engineering
    full_prompt = f"Generate {style} content with a {tone} tone. Language: {language}. Topic: {prompt}"

    try:
        response = openai.Completion.create(
            engine="text-davinci-003",
            prompt=full_prompt,
            max_tokens=500
        )
        generated_text = response.choices[0].text.strip()
        return jsonify({"content": generated_text})
    except Exception as e:
        return jsonify({"error": str(e)}), 500

@app.route("/templates", methods=["GET"])
def get_templates():
    """Provide predefined content templates."""
    templates = [
        {"name": "Blog Post", "description": "Write an engaging blog post on any topic."},
        {"name": "Social Media Ad", "description": "Create a catchy ad for social media platforms."},
        {"name": "Product Description", "description": "Generate a detailed description for a product."},
        {"name": "Email", "description": "Compose a professional email for your use case."},
    ]
    return jsonify({"templates": templates})

@app.route("/language-detect", methods=["POST"])
def detect_language():
    """Detect the language of the user-provided text."""
    text = request.json.get("text", "")
```

```
    try:
        language = detect(text)
        return jsonify({"language": language})
    except Exception as e:
        return jsonify({"error": str(e)}), 500

if __name__ == "__main__":
    app.run(debug=True)
```

Step 5: Add Advanced Features

1. Tone and Style Customization

Expand tone and style options:

- **Tones**: Friendly, professional, humorous, authoritative.
- **Styles**: Persuasive, informative, descriptive.

Add a mapping to handle these settings:

```python
Copy code
tone_map = {
    "friendly": "Write in a conversational and approachable tone.",
    "professional": "Use formal and polished language.",
    "humorous": "Make it funny and lighthearted.",
    "authoritative": "Write with confidence and expertise."
}

style_map = {
    "persuasive": "Focus on convincing the audience.",
    "informative": "Provide detailed and factual information.",
    "descriptive": "Use vivid descriptions and imagery."
}
```

Modify the generation logic:

```python
Copy code
tone_instruction = tone_map.get(tone, "Write in a neutral tone.")
style_instruction = style_map.get(style, "Write in a descriptive style.")
full_prompt = f"{tone_instruction} {style_instruction} Language: {language}.
Topic: {prompt}"
```

2. Keyword Optimization

Allow users to input keywords for SEO purposes:

```python
Copy code
```

```python
@app.route("/generate-seo", methods=["POST"])
def generate_with_keywords():
    """Generate content with keyword optimization."""
    data = request.json
    prompt = data.get("prompt", "")
    keywords = ", ".join(data.get("keywords", []))

    full_prompt = f"Write content on '{prompt}' with these keywords:
{keywords}. Ensure the keywords are used naturally."
    response = openai.Completion.create(
        engine="text-davinci-003",
        prompt=full_prompt,
        max_tokens=500
    )
    return jsonify({"content": response.choices[0].text.strip()})
```

3. Multilingual Support

Automatically translate or detect language:

```python
python
Copy code
from googletrans import Translator

translator = Translator()

@app.route("/translate", methods=["POST"])
def translate_content():
    """Translate generated content to a target language."""
    data = request.json
    text = data.get("text", "")
    target_language = data.get("target_language", "en")
    translated = translator.translate(text, dest=target_language).text
    return jsonify({"translated_text": translated})
```

Step 6: Frontend

Build a UI to interact with the API:

1. **Inputs**: Fields for prompt, tone, style, and keywords.
2. **Outputs**: Display generated content in a text editor.
3. **Templates**: Show predefined templates in a dropdown or card view.

Step 7: Deployment

- Deploy the backend to **AWS Lambda**, **Heroku**, or **Google Cloud**.
- Host the frontend using **Vercel**, **Netlify**, or similar platforms.

Future Enhancements

1. **User Authentication**: Allow users to save their preferences and generated content.
2. **Plagiarism Checker**: Integrate tools like **Copyscape** or **Turnitin**.
3. **Content History**: Store and retrieve past generated content.
4. **API for Export**: Provide options to export generated content to Word or PDF.

Chapter 16: Personalized Learning Platform

Introduction:

Personalized Learning Platform powered by a **Large Language Model (LLM)** is an excellent way to deliver customized educational experiences. These platforms can provide tailored learning paths, adaptive quizzes, and context-specific guidance based on each user's goals, progress, and preferences.

Step 1: Define the Features

Your **Personalized Learning Platform** could include:

1. **Customized Learning Paths**: Curate lessons based on user input (e.g., goals, current knowledge).
2. **Interactive Q&A**: Allow students to ask questions and receive instant answers.
3. **Topic Summarization**: Provide concise overviews of topics.
4. **Adaptive Quizzes**: Dynamically adjust question difficulty based on performance.
5. **Progress Tracking**: Track user progress and suggest areas for improvement.
6. **Multilingual Support**: Offer content and assistance in multiple languages.
7. **Gamification**: Add badges, rewards, and leaderboards for motivation.

Step 2: Choose the Technology Stack

- **Frontend**: React (web) or Flutter (mobile).
- **Backend**: Python (Flask/FastAPI).
- **Database**: PostgreSQL for user and content management.
- **LLM API**: OpenAI GPT-4, Cohere, or other LLMs.
- **Deployment**: AWS, Heroku, or Google Cloud.

Step 3: Implement Core Features

Here's a step-by-step implementation:

1. Set Up Environment

Install dependencies:

```
bash
```

```
Copy code
pip install flask openai langchain sqlalchemy
```

2. Backend Code (Flask)

Below is a Python backend for a basic personalized learning platform.

Basic Structure
```python
Copy code
from flask import Flask, request, jsonify
import openai
from sqlalchemy import create_engine, Column, Integer, String, Float
from sqlalchemy.ext.declarative import declarative_base
from sqlalchemy.orm import sessionmaker

# Initialize Flask app
app = Flask(__name__)

# OpenAI API Key
openai.api_key = "your_openai_api_key"

# Database setup
Base = declarative_base()
engine = create_engine("sqlite:///learning_platform.db")
Session = sessionmaker(bind=engine)
session = Session()

# Define User Progress Model
class UserProgress(Base):
    __tablename__ = 'user_progress'
    id = Column(Integer, primary_key=True)
    username = Column(String, unique=True, nullable=False)
    progress = Column(Float, default=0.0)

Base.metadata.create_all(engine)

# Define Routes

@app.route("/custom-path", methods=["POST"])
def custom_learning_path():
    """Generate a personalized learning path."""
    data = request.json
    subject = data.get("subject", "general knowledge")
    level = data.get("level", "beginner")

    prompt = f"Create a detailed learning path for a {level} level student in {subject}."
    response = openai.Completion.create(
        engine="text-davinci-003",
        prompt=prompt,
        max_tokens=500
    )
    return jsonify({"learning_path": response.choices[0].text.strip()})
```

```python
@app.route("/ask", methods=["POST"])
def ask_question():
    """Answer user questions interactively."""
    question = request.json.get("question", "")
    response = openai.Completion.create(
        engine="text-davinci-003",
        prompt=f"Answer this question in an educational manner: {question}",
        max_tokens=150
    )
    return jsonify({"answer": response.choices[0].text.strip()})


@app.route("/quiz", methods=["POST"])
def adaptive_quiz():
    """Generate an adaptive quiz question."""
    topic = request.json.get("topic", "general knowledge")
    difficulty = request.json.get("difficulty", "easy")

    prompt = f"Generate a {difficulty} quiz question about {topic}, with 4
multiple-choice answers and indicate the correct one."
    response = openai.Completion.create(
        engine="text-davinci-003",
        prompt=prompt,
        max_tokens=150
    )
    return jsonify({"quiz_question": response.choices[0].text.strip()})


@app.route("/progress", methods=["POST", "GET"])
def manage_progress():
    """Track and retrieve user progress."""
    if request.method == "POST":
        data = request.json
        username = data.get("username")
        progress = data.get("progress", 0.0)

        user =
session.query(UserProgress).filter_by(username=username).first()
        if user:
            user.progress = progress
        else:
            user = UserProgress(username=username, progress=progress)
            session.add(user)
        session.commit()
        return jsonify({"message": "Progress updated successfully."})

    elif request.method == "GET":
        username = request.args.get("username")
        user =
session.query(UserProgress).filter_by(username=username).first()
        if user:
            return jsonify({"username": username, "progress": user.progress})
        else:
            return jsonify({"error": "User not found."}), 404

if __name__ == "__main__":
    app.run(debug=True)
```

3. Frontend

For the frontend, you can build a user interface with the following features:

- **Login/Signup**: Let users create accounts and save progress.
- **Content Display**: Show generated learning paths and quiz questions.
- **Interactive Q&A**: Provide a chat interface for asking questions.

Step 4: Advanced Features

1. Progress Insights

Use the progress data to provide personalized recommendations:

```python
Copy code
@app.route("/recommend", methods=["POST"])
def recommend_content():
    """Recommend topics based on user progress."""
    username = request.json.get("username")
    user = session.query(UserProgress).filter_by(username=username).first()
    if not user:
        return jsonify({"error": "User not found."}), 404

    progress = user.progress
    if progress < 30:
        recommendation = "Focus on foundational topics to strengthen your
basics."
    elif progress < 70:
        recommendation = "You are doing great! Try intermediate-level
topics."
    else:
        recommendation = "You are almost an expert! Explore advanced topics
or related subjects."

    return jsonify({"recommendation": recommendation})
```

---

2. Multilingual Content

Generate learning content in different languages:

```python
Copy code
@app.route("/multilingual", methods=["POST"])
def multilingual_learning():
    """Generate content in a specified language."""
    data = request.json
```

```
subject = data.get("subject", "science")
language = data.get("language", "es")  # Default: Spanish

prompt = f"Generate an introductory lesson about {subject} in
{language}."
response = openai.Completion.create(
    engine="text-davinci-003",
    prompt=prompt,
    max_tokens=500
)
return jsonify({"lesson": response.choices[0].text.strip()})
```

Step 5: Deployment

Deploy the application using platforms like:

1. **Backend**: AWS, Heroku, or Google Cloud.
2. **Frontend**: Vercel or Netlify.

Future Enhancements

1. **Gamification**: Add badges, points, and leaderboards.
2. **Live Tutoring Integration**: Connect users with real tutors for advanced questions.
3. **Data-Driven Insights**: Use ML algorithms to analyze learning patterns.
4. **Content Export**: Allow users to download their lessons and quizzes in PDF.

Chapter No. 17 Code Generation and Debugging Tool

Introduction:

Code Generation and Debugging Tool powered by an **LLM (Large Language Model)** can be incredibly useful for developers. Such an application can assist with generating boilerplate code, solving programming challenges, refactoring, and even debugging errors in code snippets.

Step 1: Define the Features

Key features of a code generation and debugging tool include:

1. **Code Generation**: Generate boilerplate code or complete implementations based on a description.
2. **Debugging Assistance**: Analyze code and suggest fixes for errors.
3. **Code Explanation**: Explain what a specific piece of code does.
4. **Code Refactoring**: Improve the readability and maintainability of code.
5. **Multi-Language Support**: Support multiple programming languages.
6. **Integration**: Optionally integrate with IDEs (e.g., VSCode) via an API or extension.

Step 2: Choose the Technology Stack

- **Frontend**: React.js (web app) or Electron (desktop app).
- **Backend**: Python (FastAPI or Flask).
- **Database**: PostgreSQL or MongoDB for storing user data and code snippets.
- **LLM API**: OpenAI GPT-4 (or alternatives like Cohere or Anthropic Claude).
- **Deployment**: AWS, Heroku, or Azure.

Step 3: Backend Implementation

1. Set Up Environment

Install necessary libraries:

```bash
Copy code
pip install flask openai
```

2. Code for Flask Backend

Here's a basic backend implementation:

```python
Copy code
from flask import Flask, request, jsonify
import openai

# Initialize Flask app
app = Flask(__name__)

# OpenAI API Key
openai.api_key = "your_openai_api_key"

@app.route("/generate-code", methods=["POST"])
def generate_code():
    """Generate code based on a description."""
    data = request.json
    description = data.get("description", "")
    language = data.get("language", "Python")  # Default to Python

    prompt = f"Generate {language} code for: {description}"
    try:
        response = openai.Completion.create(
            engine="text-davinci-003",
            prompt=prompt,
            max_tokens=300
        )
        generated_code = response.choices[0].text.strip()
        return jsonify({"code": generated_code})
    except Exception as e:
        return jsonify({"error": str(e)}), 500

@app.route("/debug-code", methods=["POST"])
def debug_code():
    """Debug a code snippet and suggest fixes."""
    data = request.json
    code = data.get("code", "")
    language = data.get("language", "Python")

    prompt = f"Analyze and debug the following {language} code. Provide the
corrected code and explanations for fixes:\n\n{code}"
    try:
        response = openai.Completion.create(
            engine="text-davinci-003",
            prompt=prompt,
            max_tokens=500
        )
        debugged_code = response.choices[0].text.strip()
        return jsonify({"debugged_code": debugged_code})
    except Exception as e:
        return jsonify({"error": str(e)}), 500

@app.route("/explain-code", methods=["POST"])
def explain_code():
```

```python
    """Explain what the code does."""
    data = request.json
    code = data.get("code", "")

    prompt = f"Explain the functionality of the following code:\n\n{code}"
    try:
        response = openai.Completion.create(
            engine="text-davinci-003",
            prompt=prompt,
            max_tokens=300
        )
        explanation = response.choices[0].text.strip()
        return jsonify({"explanation": explanation})
    except Exception as e:
        return jsonify({"error": str(e)}), 500

@app.route("/refactor-code", methods=["POST"])
def refactor_code():
    """Refactor code for better readability and maintainability."""
    data = request.json
    code = data.get("code", "")

    prompt = f"Refactor the following code to improve its readability and
maintainability:\n\n{code}"
    try:
        response = openai.Completion.create(
            engine="text-davinci-003",
            prompt=prompt,
            max_tokens=300
        )
        refactored_code = response.choices[0].text.strip()
        return jsonify({"refactored_code": refactored_code})
    except Exception as e:
        return jsonify({"error": str(e)}), 500

if __name__ == "__main__":
    app.run(debug=True)
```

Step 4: Frontend Implementation

Create a simple user interface to interact with the API:

1. **Code Input Field**: Text area for users to input code or a problem description.
2. **Dropdown for Language**: Select programming language.
3. **Buttons for Actions**: Buttons for **Generate Code**, **Debug Code**, **Explain Code**, and **Refactor Code**.
4. **Output Area**: Display the output code or explanation.

Step 5: Advanced Features

Enhance the application with additional features:

1. Multi-Language Support

Add support for multiple programming languages:

- Modify the prompts to dynamically include the selected language.
- Provide dropdown options for languages like Python, JavaScript, Java, C++, etc.

2. Integration with IDEs

Develop an extension for IDEs like **VSCode**:

- Use the backend API to fetch results.
- Allow users to send code directly from the editor to the backend.

3. Error Classification

Provide detailed error analysis:

```python
Copy code
@app.route("/classify-error", methods=["POST"])
def classify_error():
    """Classify and explain an error in the code."""
    data = request.json
    code = data.get("code", "")
    error_message = data.get("error_message", "")

    prompt = f"Explain the following error and suggest a
fix:\n\nCode:\n{code}\n\nError:\n{error_message}"
    try:
        response = openai.Completion.create(
            engine="text-davinci-003",
            prompt=prompt,
            max_tokens=300
        )
        explanation = response.choices[0].text.strip()
        return jsonify({"explanation": explanation})
    except Exception as e:
        return jsonify({"error": str(e)}), 500
```

Step 6: Deployment

1. **Backend**: Deploy the Flask backend using **AWS Lambda**, **Heroku**, or **Google Cloud**.
2. **Frontend**: Host the web app using **Vercel**, **Netlify**, or similar services.

Step 7: Future Enhancements

1. **Code Completion**: Suggest auto-completions for partially written code.
2. **Version Control Integration**: Integrate with Git for versioning.
3. **Plagiarism Detection**: Ensure the generated code is original.
4. **Live Debugging**: Allow users to upload and debug larger projects in real-time.

Chapter No. 18 Search and Recommendation System

Introduction:

Search and Recommendation System powered by an **LLM (Large Language Model)** can offer personalized, context-aware search results and recommendations tailored to user preferences. Such a system is applicable in domains like e-commerce, content platforms, learning management systems, and more.

Step 1: Define Features

Search Features

1. **Context-Aware Search**: Use LLMs to understand the intent behind queries.
2. **Semantic Search**: Retrieve results based on meaning, not just keywords.
3. **Natural Language Queries**: Allow users to input queries in everyday language.

Recommendation Features

1. **Personalized Recommendations**: Suggest items based on user behavior and preferences.
2. **Content Similarity**: Recommend similar content/items based on a given reference.
3. **Dynamic Updates**: Update recommendations based on real-time interactions.

Step 2: Choose the Technology Stack

- **Frontend**: React.js or Vue.js for web, Flutter for mobile.
- **Backend**: Python with Flask or FastAPI.
- **Database**: MongoDB, Elasticsearch (for semantic search), or PostgreSQL.
- **LLM API**: OpenAI GPT-4 or Cohere's embedding models.
- **Deployment**: AWS, Heroku, or Google Cloud.

Step 3: Backend Implementation

1. Install Dependencies

```bash
Copy code
pip install flask openai langchain elasticsearch
```

2. Create the Backend

```python
python
Copy code
from flask import Flask, request, jsonify
import openai

app = Flask(__name__)

# OpenAI API Key
openai.api_key = "your_openai_api_key"

@app.route("/search", methods=["POST"])
def semantic_search():
    """Perform a semantic search."""
    data = request.json
    query = data.get("query", "")
    documents = data.get("documents", [])

    prompt = f"""
    Perform a semantic search. Based on the query: '{query}', rank the
following documents by relevance:
    {', '.join(documents)}
    """
    try:
        response = openai.Completion.create(
            engine="text-davinci-003",
            prompt=prompt,
            max_tokens=300
        )
        ranked_results = response.choices[0].text.strip().split("\n")
        return jsonify({"results": ranked_results})
    except Exception as e:
        return jsonify({"error": str(e)}), 500

@app.route("/recommend", methods=["POST"])
def recommend_items():
    """Provide personalized recommendations."""
    data = request.json
    user_preferences = data.get("preferences", [])
    all_items = data.get("all_items", [])

    prompt = f"""
    Given the user's preferences: {', '.join(user_preferences)}, recommend
the top 5 items from the following list:
    {', '.join(all_items)}
    """
    try:
        response = openai.Completion.create(
            engine="text-davinci-003",
            prompt=prompt,
            max_tokens=200
        )
        recommendations = response.choices[0].text.strip().split("\n")
        return jsonify({"recommendations": recommendations})
    except Exception as e:
```

```python
        return jsonify({"error": str(e)}), 500

@app.route("/similar-content", methods=["POST"])
def similar_content():
    """Find similar items based on a reference."""
    data = request.json
    reference_item = data.get("reference", "")
    items = data.get("items", [])

    prompt = f"""
Find items similar to: '{reference_item}' from the following list:
{', '.join(items)}
"""
    try:
        response = openai.Completion.create(
            engine="text-davinci-003",
            prompt=prompt,
            max_tokens=200
        )
        similar_items = response.choices[0].text.strip().split("\n")
        return jsonify({"similar_items": similar_items})
    except Exception as e:
        return jsonify({"error": str(e)}), 500

if __name__ == "__main__":
    app.run(debug=True)
```

Step 4: Frontend Implementation

Build a frontend with:

1. **Search Bar**: Allow users to input natural language queries.
2. **Recommendations Display**: Show personalized recommendations based on user preferences.
3. **Dynamic Filters**: Allow users to refine results based on categories or tags.
4. **Real-Time Updates**: Use WebSocket or polling for live updates.

Step 5: Data Preparation

For Search:

Use Elasticsearch or a similar tool to preprocess and store documents. Create embeddings using OpenAI's `text-embedding-ada-002` model:

```python
python
Copy code
import openai

def generate_embedding(text):
```

```
response = openai.Embedding.create(
    input=text,
    model="text-embedding-ada-002"
)
return response['data'][0]['embedding']
```

For Recommendations:

Maintain user profiles and interaction data in a database. Use the embeddings to calculate similarity:

```python
Copy code
from scipy.spatial.distance import cosine

def recommend(preferences, items, embeddings):
    preference_embedding = generate_embedding(preferences)
    item_scores = [(item, 1 - cosine(preference_embedding, embeddings[item]))
for item in items]
    return sorted(item_scores, key=lambda x: x[1], reverse=True)
```

Step 6: Advanced Features

1. **Real-Time Personalization**:
   o Track user clicks and searches to update recommendations dynamically.
2. **Collaborative Filtering**:
   o Use user-to-user similarity for additional recommendations.
3. **Topic Modeling**:
   o Use LLMs to cluster similar items into categories.

Step 7: Deployment

1. **Backend**: Deploy the Flask backend on **Heroku** or **AWS Lambda**.
2. **Frontend**: Host the web app using **Netlify** or **Vercel**.
3. **Data Store**: Use **Elasticsearch** for scalable document storage.

Future Enhancements

- **Cross-Domain Recommendations**: Suggest items across different domains (e.g., books and movies).
- **Voice Search**: Add voice search capabilities using a speech-to-text API.
- **Explainability**: Explain why a specific item was recommended.

Chapter No. 19 Intelligent Writing Assistant

Introduction:

Intelligent Writing Assistant using a **LLM (Large Language Model)** can revolutionize how people write by offering real-time suggestions, improving grammar, generating ideas, and enhancing the overall writing experience. This type of tool can assist in writing essays, articles, emails, or even books.

Step 1: Define the Features

Core Features

1. **Grammar and Spelling Correction**: Automatically detect and fix grammar and spelling mistakes.
2. **Sentence Structuring**: Suggest better ways to phrase sentences for clarity and flow.
3. **Text Completion**: Complete paragraphs or sentences based on a provided prompt.
4. **Tone Adjustment**: Modify the tone of the text (e.g., formal, casual, friendly, professional).
5. **Paraphrasing**: Reword sentences to avoid plagiarism or enhance expression.
6. **Idea Generation**: Suggest ideas or prompts when the user is stuck.
7. **Style Enhancement**: Suggest ways to improve the writing style for better readability.

Step 2: Choose the Technology Stack

- **Frontend**: React.js for web, Flutter for mobile apps.
- **Backend**: Python with Flask or FastAPI.
- **Database**: PostgreSQL or MongoDB for storing user history, preferences, and writing samples.
- **LLM API**: OpenAI GPT-4, Cohere, or other LLMs like Anthropic Claude.
- **Deployment**: AWS, Google Cloud, or Heroku for cloud hosting.

Step 3: Backend Implementation

1. Install Required Libraries

Install the necessary dependencies:

```bash
Copy code
pip install flask openai
```

2. Backend Code

```python
python
Copy code
from flask import Flask, request, jsonify
import openai

app = Flask(__name__)

# OpenAI API Key
openai.api_key = "your_openai_api_key"

@app.route("/grammar-correction", methods=["POST"])
def grammar_correction():
    """Correct grammar and spelling in the input text."""
    data = request.json
    text = data.get("text", "")

    prompt = f"Correct the grammar and spelling of the following
text:\n\n{text}"
    try:
        response = openai.Completion.create(
            engine="text-davinci-003",
            prompt=prompt,
            max_tokens=300
        )
        corrected_text = response.choices[0].text.strip()
        return jsonify({"corrected_text": corrected_text})
    except Exception as e:
        return jsonify({"error": str(e)}), 500

@app.route("/sentence-structuring", methods=["POST"])
def sentence_structuring():
    """Suggest improvements for sentence structure."""
    data = request.json
    sentence = data.get("sentence", "")

    prompt = f"Suggest improvements for the following sentence to enhance its
clarity and flow:\n\n{sentence}"
    try:
        response = openai.Completion.create(
            engine="text-davinci-003",
            prompt=prompt,
            max_tokens=300
        )
        improved_sentence = response.choices[0].text.strip()
        return jsonify({"improved_sentence": improved_sentence})
    except Exception as e:
        return jsonify({"error": str(e)}), 500

@app.route("/text-completion", methods=["POST"])
def text_completion():
    """Complete the text based on a provided prompt."""
    data = request.json
    prompt_text = data.get("prompt", "")
```

```python
    prompt = f"Complete the following text:\n\n{prompt_text}"
    try:
        response = openai.Completion.create(
            engine="text-davinci-003",
            prompt=prompt,
            max_tokens=200
        )
        completed_text = response.choices[0].text.strip()
        return jsonify({"completed_text": completed_text})
    except Exception as e:
        return jsonify({"error": str(e)}), 500

@app.route("/tone-adjustment", methods=["POST"])
def tone_adjustment():
    """Adjust the tone of the input text."""
    data = request.json
    text = data.get("text", "")
    desired_tone = data.get("tone", "formal")  # Example tones: formal,
casual, professional, friendly

    prompt = f"Adjust the tone of the following text to be
{desired_tone}:\n\n{text}"
    try:
        response = openai.Completion.create(
            engine="text-davinci-003",
            prompt=prompt,
            max_tokens=300
        )
        adjusted_text = response.choices[0].text.strip()
        return jsonify({"adjusted_text": adjusted_text})
    except Exception as e:
        return jsonify({"error": str(e)}), 500

@app.route("/paraphrasing", methods=["POST"])
def paraphrasing():
    """Paraphrase the input text to avoid plagiarism or enhance
expression."""
    data = request.json
    text = data.get("text", "")

    prompt = f"Paraphrase the following text to improve clarity and avoid
plagiarism:\n\n{text}"
    try:
        response = openai.Completion.create(
            engine="text-davinci-003",
            prompt=prompt,
            max_tokens=300
        )
        paraphrased_text = response.choices[0].text.strip()
        return jsonify({"paraphrased_text": paraphrased_text})
    except Exception as e:
        return jsonify({"error": str(e)}), 500

@app.route("/idea-generation", methods=["POST"])
def idea_generation():
    """Generate ideas based on a provided prompt or topic."""
    data = request.json
```

```
    topic = data.get("topic", "")

    prompt = f"Generate creative ideas or content ideas related to the
following topic:\n\n{topic}"
    try:
        response = openai.Completion.create(
            engine="text-davinci-003",
            prompt=prompt,
            max_tokens=200
        )
        ideas = response.choices[0].text.strip().split("\n")
        return jsonify({"ideas": ideas})
    except Exception as e:
        return jsonify({"error": str(e)}), 500

if __name__ == "__main__":
    app.run(debug=True)
```

Step 4: Frontend Implementation

The frontend for the writing assistant could have the following components:

1. **Text Input Area**: A large area for users to input or paste their writing.
2. **Action Buttons**: Buttons for different actions like **Correct Grammar**, **Structure Sentence**, **Complete Text**, **Adjust Tone**, **Paraphrase**, and **Generate Ideas**.
3. **Output Display**: Areas to show the corrected, improved, or completed text after the user presses an action button.
4. **Tone Selection Dropdown**: Allow users to select the tone (e.g., casual, formal).
5. **Real-Time Suggestions**: Offer inline suggestions as the user types.

Step 5: Integration with LLM

- Use **OpenAI's GPT** for generating suggestions and corrections based on the user input.
- Use **GPT-4** or **GPT-3.5-turbo** to improve performance and handle more complex writing tasks like tone adjustments or idea generation.

Step 6: Deployment

1. **Backend**: Deploy the Flask application on **Heroku** or **AWS Lambda**.
2. **Frontend**: Host the frontend using **Netlify** or **Vercel**.
3. **User Analytics**: Store user interaction data to personalize and enhance the writing assistant over time.

Future Enhancements

1. **Plagiarism Checker**: Integrate a plagiarism detection API to ensure originality.
2. **Multi-Language Support**: Support multiple languages for grammar correction and text generation.
3. **Document Templates**: Provide templates for various types of writing (e.g., emails, essays, reports).
4. **Voice Input**: Allow users to speak their writing, and convert it to text.
5. **Collaboration Features**: Allow multiple users to work together on the same document in real time.

Chapter No. 20 Healthcare Application

Introduction:

Healthcare Application using a **LLM (Large Language Model)** can significantly enhance the healthcare experience by providing medical professionals and patients with AI-powered assistance for diagnosis, symptom checking, patient interaction, mental health support, and more. Below is a step-by-step guide to building such an application.

Step 1: Define Core Features

1. Symptom Checker

- **Feature**: Allow users to input their symptoms, and the model will provide potential conditions and suggestions.
- **Functionality**: Symptom input → Diagnosis prediction → Medical advice (refer to doctor if necessary).

2. Medical Information Retrieval

- **Feature**: Help users and medical professionals retrieve medical information based on queries (e.g., drug information, disease details, treatment options).
- **Functionality**: User query → Relevant medical data retrieval from medical databases or knowledge sources.

3. Virtual Health Assistant

- **Feature**: Provide ongoing health-related advice, reminders (e.g., medication), and health monitoring (e.g., daily steps, exercise tracking).
- **Functionality**: Health status update → Personalized health tips → Wellness recommendations.

4. Mental Health Chatbot

- **Feature**: Offer conversational mental health support, such as stress management and emotional well-being tips.
- **Functionality**: User emotions → Empathetic response → Coping strategies or professional guidance.

5. Medical Documentation Automation

- **Feature**: Help doctors and healthcare professionals automate documentation tasks like generating reports, medical history summaries, and clinical notes.
- **Functionality**: Voice-to-text input → Documentation creation → Notes generation.

Step 2: Choose the Technology Stack

- **Frontend**: React.js (Web), Flutter (Mobile) for user-friendly interfaces.
- **Backend**: Flask, FastAPI, or Node.js for managing API requests.
- **Database**: MongoDB, PostgreSQL for storing user data, medical records, and other patient-related information.
- **LLM API**: OpenAI GPT-4 or Cohere API for natural language understanding and generation.
- **Medical Data Sources**: Integrate external APIs like **Medline**, **UpToDate**, or **PubMed** for reliable medical data.
- **Deployment**: AWS, Google Cloud, or Heroku for cloud hosting.

Step 3: Backend Implementation

1. Install Required Libraries

```bash
Copy code
pip install flask openai requests
```

2. Backend Code

a. Symptom Checker API

```python
Copy code
from flask import Flask, request, jsonify
import openai

app = Flask(__name__)

# OpenAI API Key
openai.api_key = "your_openai_api_key"

@app.route("/check-symptoms", methods=["POST"])
def check_symptoms():
    """Symptom checker that provides possible conditions."""
    data = request.json
    symptoms = data.get("symptoms", "")

    prompt = f"Based on the following symptoms, suggest possible medical
conditions and next steps for the patient: {symptoms}"
    try:
        response = openai.Completion.create(
            engine="text-davinci-003",
            prompt=prompt,
            max_tokens=300
        )
```

```python
        diagnosis = response.choices[0].text.strip()
        return jsonify({"diagnosis": diagnosis})
    except Exception as e:
        return jsonify({"error": str(e)}), 500


@app.route("/get-medical-info", methods=["POST"])
def get_medical_info():
    """Retrieve medical information based on user query."""
    data = request.json
    query = data.get("query", "")

    prompt = f"Provide relevant medical information regarding the following: {query}"
    try:
        response = openai.Completion.create(
            engine="text-davinci-003",
            prompt=prompt,
            max_tokens=300
        )
        info = response.choices[0].text.strip()
        return jsonify({"info": info})
    except Exception as e:
        return jsonify({"error": str(e)}), 500


@app.route("/health-assistant", methods=["POST"])
def health_assistant():
    """Provide personalized health tips and reminders."""
    data = request.json
    user_data = data.get("user_data", {})

    prompt = f"Provide personalized health tips for a person with the following health profile: {user_data}"
    try:
        response = openai.Completion.create(
            engine="text-davinci-003",
            prompt=prompt,
            max_tokens=300
        )
        health_tips = response.choices[0].text.strip()
        return jsonify({"health_tips": health_tips})
    except Exception as e:
        return jsonify({"error": str(e)}), 500


@app.route("/mental-health-chat", methods=["POST"])
def mental_health_chat():
    """Provide mental health support through chat."""
    data = request.json
    user_message = data.get("message", "")

    prompt = f"Provide mental health advice for the following conversation: {user_message}"
    try:
        response = openai.Completion.create(
            engine="text-davinci-003",
            prompt=prompt,
            max_tokens=300
        )
```

```
        response_message = response.choices[0].text.strip()
        return jsonify({"response_message": response_message})
    except Exception as e:
        return jsonify({"error": str(e)}), 500

if __name__ == "__main__":
    app.run(debug=True)
```

b. Voice-to-Text and Documentation Automation (Optional)

You can integrate voice-to-text APIs (e.g., Google Speech-to-Text) and automate documentation:

```python
Copy code
import speech_recognition as sr

def transcribe_audio_to_text(audio_file):
    recognizer = sr.Recognizer()
    with sr.AudioFile(audio_file) as source:
        audio = recognizer.record(source)
    text = recognizer.recognize_google(audio)
    return text
```

Step 4: Frontend Implementation

The frontend could include:

1. **Symptom Input Form**: A user interface where patients enter their symptoms.
2. **Medical Info Retrieval Search Bar**: Let users search for medical conditions or information.
3. **Chat Interface for Mental Health Support**: A real-time chat interface to interact with the mental health assistant.
4. **Health Tips Dashboard**: Display personalized health tips, reminders, and progress tracking.
5. **Voice Input**: Allow users to provide voice input for symptoms or health-related queries.

Step 5: Data Sources and Integration

- Integrate trusted **medical knowledge sources** to enrich your LLM-powered responses. These could include:
  - **UpToDate API**: Offers evidence-based medical information.
  - **MedlinePlus API**: Provides consumer health information from the National Library of Medicine.
  - **PubMed**: For retrieving research-based articles.

Step 6: Deployment

1. **Backend**: Deploy the Flask application on **Heroku**, **AWS Lambda**, or **Google Cloud**.
2. **Frontend**: Host the frontend using **Netlify** or **Vercel**.
3. **Medical Data Integration**: Use **AWS S3** or **Google Cloud Storage** to store large datasets like medical research.

Step 7: Future Enhancements

1. **Integration with Wearables**: Sync health data from fitness trackers (e.g., Fitbit, Apple Watch).
2. **AI-powered Diagnosis Prediction**: Use LLMs and machine learning models to assist healthcare professionals in predicting diagnoses more accurately.
3. **Telemedicine Integration**: Enable virtual consultations between patients and doctors.
4. **Privacy and Compliance**: Ensure compliance with **HIPAA** (Health Insurance Portability and Accountability Act) for data privacy and security.

Possible Use Case Example:

Patient: "I've been feeling tired, having headaches, and experiencing dizziness. What could this be?" **Assistant**: The AI-powered symptom checker could respond with:

- "These symptoms could be related to several conditions such as dehydration, anemia, or a viral infection. It's recommended to consult a healthcare professional for further evaluation."

Chapter No. 21 E-Commerce and Retail

Introduction:

E-Commerce and Retail application using an **LLM (Large Language Model)** can enhance customer experiences, improve sales processes, automate inventory management, and provide personalized recommendations. Below is a step-by-step guide to creating such an application that incorporates AI-powered functionalities.

Step 1: Define Core Features

1. Personalized Product Recommendations

- **Feature**: Provide users with personalized product suggestions based on browsing history, search queries, and preferences.
- **Functionality**: User profile → Purchase history → Personalized product recommendations.

2. Smart Search Engine

- **Feature**: Enhance search results with AI-based understanding of user queries, even handling synonyms, typos, and contextual queries.
- **Functionality**: User search input → Intelligent query processing → Relevant product suggestions.

3. Virtual Shopping Assistant

- **Feature**: Offer a conversational shopping assistant that helps customers find products, track orders, and provide product details.
- **Functionality**: User query → Product suggestion → FAQ handling → Order status.

4. Customer Support Chatbot

- **Feature**: Automate customer service interactions for inquiries about products, returns, exchanges, and troubleshooting.
- **Functionality**: Customer query → Relevant answer generation → Escalation to human support if necessary.

5. Inventory Management

- **Feature**: AI-powered predictions for stock management, such as restocking recommendations based on sales trends and demand forecasting.
- **Functionality**: Product sales data → Restocking recommendations → Inventory reports.

6. Review and Sentiment Analysis

- **Feature**: Analyze customer reviews to identify sentiment and trends, providing actionable insights.
- **Functionality**: Customer reviews → Sentiment analysis → Actionable insights (e.g., product improvements).

7. Fraud Detection

- **Feature**: Use AI models to detect suspicious patterns of behavior and potential fraudulent transactions.
- **Functionality**: Purchase patterns → Fraud detection alerts → Transaction verification.

Step 2: Choose the Technology Stack

- **Frontend**: React.js (Web), Flutter (Mobile) for a responsive and user-friendly UI.
- **Backend**: Python with Flask/FastAPI or Node.js for managing requests.
- **Database**: MongoDB or PostgreSQL for storing product data, user profiles, order history, and inventory.
- **LLM API**: OpenAI GPT-4 or Cohere for intelligent natural language processing.
- **Search Engine**: Elasticsearch for powerful, AI-enhanced search functionality.
- **Deployment**: AWS, Google Cloud, or Heroku for cloud hosting and scalability.

Step 3: Backend Implementation

1. Install Required Libraries

Install the necessary dependencies:

```bash
Copy code
pip install flask openai elasticsearch
```

2. Backend Code for Key Features

a. Personalized Product Recommendations

```python
Copy code
from flask import Flask, request, jsonify
import openai

app = Flask(__name__)

# OpenAI API Key
openai.api_key = "your_openai_api_key"
```

117

```python
@app.route("/recommend-products", methods=["POST"])
def recommend_products():
    """Generate personalized product recommendations based on user
preferences."""
    data = request.json
    user_profile = data.get("user_profile", {})

    prompt = f"Generate product recommendations for a user with the following
profile: {user_profile}"
    try:
        response = openai.Completion.create(
            engine="text-davinci-003",
            prompt=prompt,
            max_tokens=300
        )
        recommendations = response.choices[0].text.strip().split("\n")
        return jsonify({"recommendations": recommendations})
    except Exception as e:
        return jsonify({"error": str(e)}), 500
```

b. Smart Search Engine

```python
python
Copy code
from flask import Flask, request, jsonify
from elasticsearch import Elasticsearch

app = Flask(__name__)

# Initialize Elasticsearch
es = Elasticsearch([{'host': 'localhost', 'port': 9200}])

@app.route("/search-products", methods=["POST"])
def search_products():
    """Search for products based on user query."""
    data = request.json
    query = data.get("query", "")

    body = {
        "query": {
            "multi_match": {
                "query": query,
                "fields": ["product_name", "product_description"]
            }
        }
    }
    try:
        result = es.search(index="products", body=body)
        products = [hit["_source"] for hit in result["hits"]["hits"]]
        return jsonify({"products": products})
    except Exception as e:
        return jsonify({"error": str(e)}), 500
```

c. Virtual Shopping Assistant

```python
python
Copy code
```

```python
@app.route("/shopping-assistant", methods=["POST"])
def shopping_assistant():
    """Assist with finding products, tracking orders, and providing product
details."""
    data = request.json
    user_query = data.get("query", "")

    prompt = f"Assist the user with the following query: {user_query}"
    try:
        response = openai.Completion.create(
            engine="text-davinci-003",
            prompt=prompt,
            max_tokens=300
        )
        assistant_response = response.choices[0].text.strip()
        return jsonify({"response": assistant_response})
    except Exception as e:
        return jsonify({"error": str(e)}), 500
```

d. Customer Support Chatbot

```python
python
Copy code
@app.route("/customer-support", methods=["POST"])
def customer_support():
    """Provide automated customer support for product inquiries, returns,
etc."""
    data = request.json
    customer_query = data.get("query", "")

    prompt = f"Answer the following customer query: {customer_query}"
    try:
        response = openai.Completion.create(
            engine="text-davinci-003",
            prompt=prompt,
            max_tokens=300
        )
        support_response = response.choices[0].text.strip()
        return jsonify({"response": support_response})
    except Exception as e:
        return jsonify({"error": str(e)}), 500
```

Step 4: Frontend Implementation

The frontend could include:

1. **Product Search Bar**: Let users search for products with intelligent query handling.
2. **Recommendation Carousel**: Show personalized product recommendations based on browsing or purchase history.
3. **Chat Interface**: Provide a chatbot for customer service and virtual shopping assistance.
4. **Product Details Page**: Display detailed product information, reviews, and an option to ask questions about the product.
5. **Order Status Page**: Allow users to track the status of their orders in real-time.

6. **User Dashboard**: Provide a personalized space for users to manage their profiles, order history, and preferences.

Step 5: Integrating with AI-powered Features

- **Product Recommendations**: Use **OpenAI GPT-4** or **GPT-3** for generating personalized recommendations based on user preferences and history.
- **Customer Support**: Use the same LLM for providing automated customer service answers to common queries.
- **Search Engine**: Use **Elasticsearch** to enhance the search capabilities, ensuring it understands synonyms, product variations, and contextual queries.
- **Inventory Management**: You can build AI models using historical sales data to predict when to restock products.

Step 6: Deployment

1. **Backend**: Host the backend API on **Heroku**, **AWS Lambda**, or **Google Cloud**.
2. **Frontend**: Host the frontend UI on **Netlify** or **Vercel** for fast deployment and scalability.
3. **Database**: Use **MongoDB** or **PostgreSQL** for storing user data, product inventory, and transactional information.
4. **Search Engine**: Set up **Elasticsearch** for advanced product search capabilities.

Step 7: Future Enhancements

1. **Voice Shopping**: Enable voice-based interactions for shopping assistance, allowing users to shop hands-free.
2. **AI for Pricing Optimization**: Use AI to recommend dynamic pricing strategies based on market trends, competitor pricing, and demand.
3. **Real-time Order Tracking**: Offer real-time updates on shipping status using APIs from shipping providers (e.g., FedEx, UPS).
4. **Social Media Integration**: Leverage social media posts and sentiment analysis to personalize product recommendations.
5. **Augmented Reality (AR)**: Integrate AR for virtual try-ons of products like clothes or accessories.

Example Use Case:

Customer: "I'm looking for a red dress for a wedding." **Assistant**: The virtual shopping assistant powered by the LLM could respond with:

- "Here are some options for red dresses that are perfect for weddings: [Product 1], [Product 2], [Product 3]. Would you like to see more details or refine your search?"

Chapter No. 22 Legal and Financial Assistants

Introduction:

Legal and Financial Assistants using an **LLM (Large Language Model)** can be incredibly beneficial, providing services like contract analysis, legal document drafting, financial advice, budgeting, and more. Below is a step-by-step guide to building an application powered by LLMs to assist with both legal and financial tasks.

Step 1: Define Core Features for Legal and Financial Assistants

Legal Assistant Features

1. **Contract Drafting & Review**: Generate legal documents such as contracts, NDAs, and agreements, or assist in reviewing existing documents.
   - **Functionality**: User inputs document type, specific clauses, and details → AI drafts or reviews the document.
2. **Legal Research**: Provide summaries of case law, statutes, and legal principles related to a particular subject.
   - **Functionality**: User query about a legal topic → AI generates a concise summary or points to relevant cases or laws.
3. **Compliance Assistance**: Help businesses ensure they follow the legal regulations relevant to their industry.
   - **Functionality**: User inputs industry and jurisdiction → AI outlines compliance requirements.
4. **Legal Advice**: Answer legal questions related to various topics, such as intellectual property, contracts, and corporate law.
   - **Functionality**: User asks legal question → AI generates contextually accurate advice based on existing law.

Financial Assistant Features

1. **Financial Planning & Budgeting**: Help users create a financial plan and track expenses based on their goals.
   - **Functionality**: User inputs income, expenses, and goals → AI creates a customized financial plan.
2. **Investment Advice**: Provide general financial advice on investments like stocks, mutual funds, etc.
   - **Functionality**: User inputs investment goals → AI suggests a diversified investment strategy.
3. **Tax Calculations & Planning**: Help users calculate taxes and create a plan to optimize their tax liabilities.

- - **Functionality**: User inputs income and deductions → AI estimates taxes and suggests tax-saving strategies.
4. **Debt Management**: Provide advice on managing and reducing debts, including strategies like debt snowball or avalanche.
   - **Functionality**: User inputs debt amounts and interest rates → AI suggests a repayment plan.
5. **Financial Report Generation**: Automatically generate financial summaries and reports based on input data.
   - **Functionality**: User provides financial data → AI generates summary reports or forecasts.

Step 2: Choose the Technology Stack

- **Frontend**: React.js (Web), Flutter (Mobile) for responsive UI.
- **Backend**: Python with Flask/FastAPI or Node.js for managing requests.
- **Database**: PostgreSQL or MongoDB for storing documents, user data, and financial records.
- **LLM API**: OpenAI GPT-4, Cohere, or other LLMs for text generation and legal/financial advice.
- **Deployment**: AWS, Google Cloud, or Heroku for cloud hosting and scalability.

Step 3: Backend Implementation

1. Install Required Libraries

```bash
Copy code
pip install flask openai
```

2. Backend Code for Key Features

a. Contract Drafting & Review

```python
Copy code
from flask import Flask, request, jsonify
import openai

app = Flask(__name__)

# OpenAI API Key
openai.api_key = "your_openai_api_key"

@app.route("/draft-contract", methods=["POST"])
def draft_contract():
    """Draft a contract based on user input."""
    data = request.json
```

```python
    contract_details = data.get("contract_details", "")

    prompt = f"Draft a legal contract based on the following details:
{contract_details}"
    try:
        response = openai.Completion.create(
            engine="text-davinci-003",
            prompt=prompt,
            max_tokens=500
        )
        contract = response.choices[0].text.strip()
        return jsonify({"contract": contract})
    except Exception as e:
        return jsonify({"error": str(e)}), 500
```

b. Legal Research

```python
python
Copy code
@app.route("/legal-research", methods=["POST"])
def legal_research():
    """Perform legal research based on user query."""
    data = request.json
    legal_query = data.get("legal_query", "")

    prompt = f"Provide a summary of legal principles or case law for the
following query: {legal_query}"
    try:
        response = openai.Completion.create(
            engine="text-davinci-003",
            prompt=prompt,
            max_tokens=500
        )
        legal_summary = response.choices[0].text.strip()
        return jsonify({"legal_summary": legal_summary})
    except Exception as e:
        return jsonify({"error": str(e)}), 500
```

c. Financial Planning & Budgeting

```python
python
Copy code
@app.route("/financial-plan", methods=["POST"])
def financial_plan():
    """Create a personalized financial plan based on user data."""
    data = request.json
    income = data.get("income", 0)
    expenses = data.get("expenses", [])
    financial_goals = data.get("goals", "")

    prompt = f"Create a financial plan for someone with an income of {income}
and the following expenses: {expenses}. Their financial goals are:
{financial_goals}."
    try:
        response = openai.Completion.create(
            engine="text-davinci-003",
            prompt=prompt,
            max_tokens=500
```

```python
    )
        plan = response.choices[0].text.strip()
        return jsonify({"financial_plan": plan})
    except Exception as e:
        return jsonify({"error": str(e)}), 500
```

d. Investment Advice

```python
python
Copy code
@app.route("/investment-advice", methods=["POST"])
def investment_advice():
    """Generate investment advice based on user input."""
    data = request.json
    investment_goals = data.get("investment_goals", "")
    risk_tolerance = data.get("risk_tolerance", "medium")

    prompt = f"Provide investment advice for someone with the following
goals: {investment_goals} and a risk tolerance of {risk_tolerance}."
    try:
        response = openai.Completion.create(
            engine="text-davinci-003",
            prompt=prompt,
            max_tokens=500
        )
        advice = response.choices[0].text.strip()
        return jsonify({"investment_advice": advice})
    except Exception as e:
        return jsonify({"error": str(e)}), 500
```

e. Tax Calculation & Planning

```python
python
Copy code
@app.route("/tax-planning", methods=["POST"])
def tax_planning():
    """Help users with tax calculations and planning strategies."""
    data = request.json
    income = data.get("income", 0)
    deductions = data.get("deductions", 0)

    prompt = f"Calculate the tax for someone with an income of {income} and
the following deductions: {deductions}. Provide strategies to reduce tax
liabilities."
    try:
        response = openai.Completion.create(
            engine="text-davinci-003",
            prompt=prompt,
            max_tokens=500
        )
        tax_info = response.choices[0].text.strip()
        return jsonify({"tax_info": tax_info})
    except Exception as e:
        return jsonify({"error": str(e)}), 500
```

Step 4: Frontend Implementation

The frontend could include:

1. **Contract Assistant**: A form where users input contract details and receive a draft contract.
2. **Legal Query Search**: A search bar where users can ask legal questions, receiving summaries or relevant case law.
3. **Financial Planning Dashboard**: An interactive page where users can input their financial data and view personalized plans and advice.
4. **Investment Recommendations**: A page where users can input investment preferences and receive tailored investment strategies.
5. **Tax Planning Calculator**: A tool that lets users input their financial details to calculate taxes and receive planning advice.

Step 5: Integrating with AI-powered Features

- **Contract Drafting**: Use OpenAI models to generate detailed contracts with the required clauses.
- **Legal Research**: Use GPT-3 or GPT-4 to extract summaries and relevant case law for specific legal queries.
- **Financial Advice**: Use GPT models to provide personalized financial advice based on goals and current financial situations.
- **Investment Strategies**: Offer personalized investment suggestions by analyzing user goals and risk tolerance.
- **Tax Planning**: Calculate taxes and suggest savings strategies using AI.

Step 6: Deployment

1. **Backend**: Host the backend API on **AWS Lambda**, **Heroku**, or **Google Cloud**.
2. **Frontend**: Host the frontend UI on **Netlify** or **Vercel** for easy deployment and scalability.
3. **Database**: Use **MongoDB** or **PostgreSQL** to store user financial data and documents.
4. **AI Model**: Host the LLM model on **OpenAI's API** or use a local model if needed for large-scale applications.

Step 7: Future Enhancements

1. **Voice-based Interaction**: Enable users to interact with the assistant via voice, making it more accessible.
2. **AI Legal Assistant for Litigation**: Add the capability to analyze legal documents for potential litigation strategies.
3. **Automated Reporting**: Provide automated, easy-to-read financial reports that give users a snapshot of their finances.

4. **Blockchain Integration**: Integrate blockchain for secure and verifiable financial transactions or legal contracts.

Example Use Case:

User: "I need a contract for a non-disclosure agreement (NDA)." **Assistant**: "Please provide the details of the NDA (parties involved, duration, confidentiality clauses)." **User**: "The NDA is between Company A and Company B, lasting for 3 years, covering intellectual property and trade secrets." **Assistant**: "Here is your NDA draft based on the provided details: [Generated Contract]."

Chapter No. 23 Multimodal applications

Introduction:

Multimodal applications using **LLMs (Large Language Models)** involves integrating various input types like text, images, audio, and even video, to make applications more interactive and capable of understanding complex user requests. For instance, applications could combine text-based input with images for more accurate content generation or provide richer interactions like voice-controlled systems that interpret both spoken and visual cues.

Let's break down the process of developing a multimodal application using an **LLM** model.

Step 1: Define the Core Features of the Multimodal Application

Key Features for Multimodal Applications

1. **Image-to-Text Generation (Image Captioning)**: Convert images into detailed text descriptions. Useful for accessibility, search engines, and content creation.
   - **Functionality**: User uploads an image → AI generates a detailed textual description.
2. **Text-to-Image Generation**: Generate images based on textual descriptions. For example, generating illustrations from a scene description.
   - **Functionality**: User inputs a description → AI generates an image based on the text.
3. **Speech-to-Text Conversion**: Convert voice inputs into text for user interactions, assisting in hands-free operations.
   - **Functionality**: User speaks → AI converts speech into text for further processing.
4. **Text-to-Speech**: Convert text into natural speech output for accessibility and voice-based assistants.
   - **Functionality**: AI reads text aloud based on user input.
5. **Multimodal Chatbots**: Chatbots capable of processing multiple input types such as voice, images, and text to respond intelligently.
   - **Functionality**: User communicates via text, voice, or images → AI responds using the most appropriate modality.
6. **Video Summarization and Query Answering**: Analyze video content to generate summaries or answer user queries based on the video content.
   - **Functionality**: User uploads a video → AI processes the video to summarize key information or answer questions about the content.

Step 2: Choose the Technology Stack

- **Frontend**:
  - o React or Angular for web-based UIs.
  - o Flutter or React Native for mobile platforms.
  - o WebRTC for live video/audio streaming.
- **Backend**:
  - o Python with Flask or FastAPI for API endpoints.
  - o TensorFlow, PyTorch for multimodal model training and fine-tuning.
  - o OpenAI GPT-4, CLIP, or other multimodal models like DALL·E for image-to-text and text-to-image processing.
- **Database**:
  - o MongoDB or PostgreSQL to store images, text, user data, and metadata.
- **Multimodal Processing APIs**:
  - o OpenAI API for GPT-4 and DALL·E for text-to-image generation and understanding.
  - o Google Cloud Vision for image recognition.
  - o Amazon Transcribe for speech-to-text services.
- **Deployment**:
  - o AWS, Google Cloud, or Microsoft Azure for cloud-based deployment.
  - o Docker for containerized deployment of multimodal models.

Step 3: Backend Development (API Layer)

For multimodal applications, you need to handle various input types (text, image, audio). The backend needs to be capable of processing these inputs and invoking the appropriate models.

1. Install Required Libraries

```bash
Copy code
pip install flask openai google-cloud-vision amazon-transcribe
```

2. Implement Backend Endpoints for Each Modality

a. Image-to-Text Generation (Image Captioning)

Using **Google Vision API** for image recognition and **OpenAI GPT-4** for descriptive text generation.

```python
Copy code
from flask import Flask, request, jsonify
import openai
from google.cloud import vision

app = Flask(__name__)

# OpenAI and Google Cloud Vision setup
```

```
openai.api_key = "your_openai_api_key"
vision_client = vision.ImageAnnotatorClient()

@app.route("/image-to-text", methods=["POST"])
def image_to_text():
    """Convert image to text description."""
    file = request.files['image']

    # Perform OCR with Google Vision
    image = vision.Image(content=file.read())
    response = vision_client.label_detection(image=image)

    labels = [label.description for label in response.label_annotations]
    image_description = f"The image contains: {', '.join(labels)}."

    return jsonify({"description": image_description})
```

b. Text-to-Image Generation

Using **DALL·E** (or any similar model like Stable Diffusion) to generate images from a text prompt.

```
python
Copy code
@app.route("/text-to-image", methods=["POST"])
def text_to_image():
    """Generate an image from text."""
    data = request.json
    text_prompt = data.get("text_prompt", "")

    try:
        response = openai.Image.create(
            prompt=text_prompt,
            n=1,
            size="1024x1024"
        )
        image_url = response['data'][0]['url']
        return jsonify({"image_url": image_url})
    except Exception as e:
        return jsonify({"error": str(e)}), 500
```

c. Speech-to-Text Conversion

Using **Amazon Transcribe** to convert voice input into text.

```
python
Copy code
import boto3

transcribe_client = boto3.client('transcribe', region_name='us-east-1')

@app.route("/speech-to-text", methods=["POST"])
def speech_to_text():
    """Convert speech to text."""
    file = request.files['audio']
```

```python
    # Upload audio to AWS S3
    s3 = boto3.client('s3')
    s3.upload_fileobj(file, 'your-s3-bucket', 'audio.wav')

    # Start transcription job
    job_name = 'your-job-name'
    transcribe_client.start_transcription_job(
        TranscriptionJobName=job_name,
        Media={'MediaFileUri': f"s3://your-s3-bucket/audio.wav"},
        MediaFormat='wav',
        LanguageCode='en-US'
    )

    # Poll for job completion
    result =
transcribe_client.get_transcription_job(TranscriptionJobName=job_name)

    if result['TranscriptionJob']['TranscriptionJobStatus'] == 'COMPLETED':
        transcript_url =
result['TranscriptionJob']['Transcript']['TranscriptFileUri']
        return jsonify({"transcript_url": transcript_url})
    else:
        return jsonify({"error": "Transcription job failed"}), 500
```

d. Text-to-Speech Conversion

Using **Google Cloud Text-to-Speech** API to convert text to speech.

```python
python
Copy code
from google.cloud import texttospeech

client = texttospeech.TextToSpeechClient()

@app.route("/text-to-speech", methods=["POST"])
def text_to_speech():
    """Convert text to speech."""
    data = request.json
    text = data.get("text", "")

    input_text = texttospeech.SynthesisInput(text=text)
    voice = texttospeech.VoiceSelectionParams(language_code="en-US",
ssml_gender=texttospeech.SsmlVoiceGender.NEUTRAL)
    audio_config =
texttospeech.AudioConfig(audio_encoding=texttospeech.AudioEncoding.MP3)

    response = client.synthesize_speech(input=input_text, voice=voice,
audio_config=audio_config)

    return jsonify({"audio_content":
response.audio_content.decode("base64")})
```

A chatbot capable of processing both text and images and responding accordingly.

```python
Copy code
@app.route("/multimodal-chat", methods=["POST"])
def multimodal_chat():
    """Handle multimodal chat (text + images)."""
    data = request.json
    text_query = data.get("text_query", "")
    image_file = data.get("image", None)

    # Process text
    response_text = openai.Completion.create(
        engine="text-davinci-003",
        prompt=text_query,
        max_tokens=150
    )

    # Process image (if provided)
    if image_file:
        image = vision.Image(content=image_file)
        vision_response = vision_client.label_detection(image=image)
        labels = [label.description for label in
vision_response.label_annotations]
        image_description = f"Image contains: {', '.join(labels)}."
    else:
        image_description = ""

    return jsonify({
        "text_response": response_text.choices[0].text.strip(),
        "image_description": image_description
    })
```

Step 4: Frontend Implementation

Frontend Components

1. **Text Input Field**: Allows users to enter text for various functionalities like text-to-image, multimodal chat, etc.
2. **Voice Input (Microphone Button)**: Users can speak, and the app will convert speech into text for processing.
3. **Image Upload**: A button to upload images that the application will process.
4. **Multimodal Chat**: A chat interface where users can input text and images to interact with the AI.
5. **Output Area**: Display responses from the model (text, generated images, or audio).

Step 5: Deployment

1. **Backend Hosting**: Deploy backend APIs on platforms like **AWS Lambda**, **Google Cloud Functions**, or **Heroku**.
2. **Frontend Hosting**: Host your front-end on **Netlify, Vercel**, or **AWS S3**.
3. **Multimodal Models**: Use cloud services to host multimodal models like **DALL·E** for text-to-image or **CLIP** for vision tasks.

Step 6: Future Enhancements

1. **Voice-activated Control**: Allow users to interact with the application using voice commands for a more seamless experience.
2. **Real-time Processing**: Implement real-time voice and video processing for interactive video calls or live captioning.
3. **Advanced Multimodal AI**: Integrate models that process video and audio together to create richer interactions.

Example Use Case:

User: "Can you create an image of a mountain with a lake?" **Assistant**: "Sure! Here's your generated image: [Image]."

User: "What does this picture show?" (Uploads an image of a cat) **Assistant**: "This image contains a cat."

Chapter No. 24 Enterprise tools

Introduction:

Enterprise tools using **LLMs (Large Language Models)** involves designing applications that help businesses streamline operations, improve efficiency, and leverage AI for decision-making, automation, and data analysis. These tools can be applied across various business functions, including customer support, HR, sales, marketing, business intelligence, and more.

Let's explore how you can create a suite of **enterprise tools** using LLMs:

Step 1: Define Core Enterprise Tools and Features

Here are a few key enterprise tools that can be powered by LLMs:

1. **Automated Customer Support**
   o **Functionality**: Handle customer inquiries, complaints, and frequently asked questions (FAQs) using AI-powered chatbots. Can be integrated into websites or CRM tools to provide immediate responses.
   o **LLM Capabilities**: Understand and respond to customer questions, manage workflows, generate ticket summaries, and escalate issues as necessary.
2. **Document Automation & Summarization**
   o **Functionality**: Automatically generate, summarize, or extract key information from business documents like contracts, reports, emails, and proposals.
   o **LLM Capabilities**: Text summarization, entity recognition, document analysis, and content generation.
3. **Intelligent HR Assistant**
   o **Functionality**: Assist HR departments by automating repetitive tasks, including recruitment, employee inquiries, performance review generation, and training recommendations.
   o **LLM Capabilities**: Answer HR-related questions, assist in writing job descriptions, help with onboarding processes, and manage leave requests.
4. **Sales Enablement Tools**
   o **Functionality**: Help sales teams generate personalized email responses, product recommendations, and manage customer interactions.
   o **LLM Capabilities**: Analyze customer data to generate personalized responses, sales proposals, and follow-ups. Integrate with CRM systems like Salesforce to assist with lead management and outreach.
5. **Business Intelligence and Reporting Tools**
   o **Functionality**: Analyze company data (e.g., sales, financial, marketing) and generate insights, visualizations, and actionable reports. The AI can provide summaries of key performance indicators (KPIs) or generate forecasts.
   o **LLM Capabilities**: Summarize complex datasets, generate reports based on user queries, assist in financial analysis, and provide insights into trends.

6. **Legal Document Processing**
   - **Functionality**: Automatically analyze legal contracts, NDAs, and other documents, extract key clauses, and provide risk assessments.
   - **LLM Capabilities**: Contract analysis, clause extraction, legal advice generation, and risk prediction.
7. **Project Management Assistance**
   - **Functionality**: Assist in project planning, progress tracking, task delegation, and risk management. It can automate meeting notes, action items, and follow-ups.
   - **LLM Capabilities**: Summarize meeting notes, suggest task priorities, generate project timelines, and analyze project status reports.

Step 2: Choose the Technology Stack

Frontend Technologies:

- React, Angular, or Vue.js for dynamic user interfaces.
- Material-UI or Bootstrap for enterprise-grade design systems.
- Data visualization libraries like Chart.js, D3.js, or Plotly for generating business dashboards.

Backend Technologies:

- **Python** (Flask, Django, or FastAPI) for API services and LLM integrations.
- **Node.js** for handling real-time data and API communication.
- **Rasa** or **Dialogflow** for chatbot development.
- **Hugging Face Transformers** or **OpenAI API** for LLM-based text generation, summarization, and question-answering.

Database:

- PostgreSQL or MySQL for structured data storage.
- MongoDB for unstructured data or document storage.
- Redis or Elasticsearch for fast search capabilities.

AI and NLP Libraries:

- **Hugging Face Transformers**: For utilizing models like GPT, BERT, or custom-trained models for various LLM tasks.
- **spaCy**: For named entity recognition (NER) and document parsing.
- **OpenAI API**: For text generation and processing capabilities.

Deployment:

- **AWS**, **Google Cloud**, or **Microsoft Azure** for scalable cloud infrastructure.
- **Docker** for containerizing the application and ensuring easy deployment across environments.

- **Kubernetes** for managing and orchestrating containerized applications in production.

Step 3: Backend Development (API Layer)

Let's consider a few key enterprise tools and their corresponding API designs.

a. Automated Customer Support (Chatbot)

The goal here is to provide AI-based customer support that can automatically handle basic inquiries and escalate more complex issues to human agents.

API Endpoint Example:

```python
python
Copy code
from flask import Flask, request, jsonify
import openai

app = Flask(__name__)

# Set OpenAI API Key
openai.api_key = "your_openai_api_key"

@app.route("/customer-support", methods=["POST"])
def customer_support():
    """Handle customer support queries."""
    data = request.json
    query = data.get("query", "")

    # Use LLM (OpenAI GPT) to process the query
    response = openai.Completion.create(
        engine="davinci-codex",  # Or "gpt-3.5-turbo"
        prompt=f"Answer this customer query: {query}",
        max_tokens=150
    )

    # Return AI's response
    return jsonify({"response": response.choices[0].text.strip()})
```

---

b. Document Summarization Tool

This API will automatically summarize long documents (such as business reports) and extract key insights.

```python
python
Copy code
@app.route("/summarize-document", methods=["POST"])
def summarize_document():
    """Summarize business documents."""
```

```python
    file = request.files['document']
    text = extract_text_from_document(file)  # Custom function to extract
text from PDF/Word

    # Summarize the extracted text using LLM (GPT-4)
    response = openai.Completion.create(
        engine="gpt-4",
        prompt=f"Summarize the following document: {text}",
        max_tokens=300
    )

    return jsonify({"summary": response.choices[0].text.strip()})
```

c. Intelligent HR Assistant

An HR assistant that can help HR teams by generating job descriptions, handling employee queries, and assisting with onboarding.

```python
Copy code
@app.route("/hr-assistant", methods=["POST"])
def hr_assistant():
    """Assist with HR tasks."""
    data = request.json
    query = data.get("query", "")

    # Use GPT model to answer HR-related queries
    response = openai.Completion.create(
        engine="davinci-codex",
        prompt=f"HR Assistant: {query}",
        max_tokens=200
    )

    return jsonify({"response": response.choices[0].text.strip()})
```

d. Sales Proposal Generator

Generate personalized proposals for clients based on customer details, project needs, and preferred products.

```python
Copy code
@app.route("/generate-proposal", methods=["POST"])
def generate_proposal():
    """Generate personalized sales proposals."""
    data = request.json
    customer_name = data.get("customer_name")
    project_description = data.get("project_description")
    products = data.get("products")

    # Generate proposal using LLM (GPT-4)
    prompt = f"Create a sales proposal for {customer_name} based on the
following details: {project_description}. Products: {', '.join(products)}"
```

```
response = openai.Completion.create(
    engine="gpt-4",
    prompt=prompt,
    max_tokens=500
)

return jsonify({"proposal": response.choices[0].text.strip()})
```

Step 4: Frontend Implementation

- **Dashboard for Monitoring**: A central dashboard where administrators can monitor AI-powered activities (e.g., ticket status, HR tasks, etc.), performance analytics, and insights.
- **Dynamic Forms**: For users to input business-related queries or upload documents for analysis.
- **Chat Interface**: A chat interface to interact with the AI-powered assistant in real-time.
- **Report Visualization**: Display AI-generated reports and summaries with visualization tools like charts or graphs.

Step 5: Deployment

1. **API Hosting**: Deploy the backend APIs on cloud platforms like AWS Lambda or Google Cloud Functions.
2. **Web Hosting**: Host the front-end dashboard on platforms like AWS S3, Vercel, or Netlify.
3. **Model Hosting**: You can host custom-trained models on cloud-based AI services like AWS SageMaker or Google AI Platform.

Step 6: Scaling and Maintenance

- **Load Balancing**: Use auto-scaling groups and load balancers (AWS Elastic Load Balancer) to handle varying workloads.
- **Model Fine-tuning**: As your enterprise tools accumulate more data, fine-tune models to improve performance on specific business tasks.
- **Regular Updates**: Regularly update the models and backend infrastructure for improved features and security.

Example Use Case

1. HR Assistant:

HR managers can ask the LLM-powered assistant to generate job descriptions based on a set of criteria, process employee queries (e.g., "How many sick days are left for John?"), and assist with onboarding new employees.

User: "Create a job description for a software engineer specializing in AI." **Assistant**: "Here's the job description: [Detailed description generated]."

2. Document Automation:

A legal team can use the document automation tool to summarize legal documents and extract key clauses.

User: "Summarize the key clauses of this NDA." **Assistant**: "Here's a summary of the NDA: [Summary generated]."

Chapter No. 25 Gaming and Entertainment applications

Introduction:

Gaming and Entertainment applications powered by **LLMs (Large Language Models)** can significantly enhance the user experience by providing interactive, dynamic content, intelligent NPCs (Non-Player Characters), game storytelling, and personalized experiences. These applications can also leverage LLMs for content generation, user engagement, and storytelling, making the gaming experience more immersive.

Let's walk through how you can create a **Gaming and Entertainment application** using LLMs.

Step 1: Define Core Features for Gaming and Entertainment

Here are some key features that an LLM-powered gaming and entertainment application could offer:

1. Dynamic Game Storytelling and Dialogue Systems

- **Functionality**: Use LLMs to create adaptive dialogue systems where NPCs (Non-Player Characters) respond to players' actions and inputs in real-time, allowing for branching narratives and personalized storylines.
- **LLM Capabilities**: Understand player inputs, dynamically generate responses, and adjust the story based on player choices.

2. Procedural Content Generation (PCG)

- **Functionality**: Automatically generate game worlds, quests, characters, and narratives based on player interactions and game progress.
- **LLM Capabilities**: Generate dynamic descriptions of locations, quests, and characters, and adapt content based on player preferences or behavior.

3. AI Dungeon Master (DM) for Tabletop Games

- **Functionality**: In tabletop role-playing games (RPGs), LLMs can serve as an AI Dungeon Master that creates scenarios, quests, and encounters, and guides players through the game world.
- **LLM Capabilities**: Handle rule interpretation, create scenarios on the fly, and adapt storylines based on player decisions.

4. Game Character Customization and Interaction

- **Functionality**: Players can interact with in-game characters who can offer personalized responses, backstories, and even evolve based on the player's actions.

- **LLM Capabilities**: Allow NPCs to have in-depth personalities, memories, and evolving relationships with players.

5. Game-Based AI Companions

- **Functionality**: Create in-game companions powered by LLMs that assist players by offering hints, forming relationships, and providing advice or companionship during gameplay.
- **LLM Capabilities**: Provide dynamic dialogue, emotional intelligence, and adjust behavior based on player interactions.

6. Interactive Fiction and Visual Novels

- **Functionality**: Create interactive fiction games or visual novels where the narrative adapts in real-time to the player's choices and actions.
- **LLM Capabilities**: Generate unique dialogue options, plot twists, and character interactions based on player input.

7. Personalized Game Recommendations

- **Functionality**: Suggest personalized games, quests, or in-game content based on player preferences, playstyle, and history.
- **LLM Capabilities**: Analyze player data and recommend content such as quests, missions, or even new games based on their interests.

Step 2: Choose Technology Stack

Frontend Technologies:

- **Unity or Unreal Engine** for game development and rendering.
- **React** or **Vue.js** for web-based interactive fiction or visual novels.
- **Godot Engine** or **CryEngine** for 2D/3D game development with potential integration with LLMs for text-based interactions.

Backend Technologies:

- **Python** (Flask, Django, or FastAPI) for API development and AI integration.
- **Node.js** for handling real-time data and interactions in multiplayer or online games.
- **Socket.IO** or **WebRTC** for real-time multiplayer game communication.

Database:

- **MongoDB** for storing user data, game progress, NPC behaviors, and dynamic content.
- **PostgreSQL** for structured data storage, such as user profiles and game metadata.

AI and NLP Libraries:

- **Hugging Face Transformers**: Use models like GPT for generating dialogue and story content.
- **OpenAI API**: Use GPT or other models to power dynamic game content generation.
- **spaCy** or **NLTK**: For additional text processing, like sentiment analysis or character trait extraction.

Deployment:

- **AWS**, **Google Cloud**, or **Microsoft Azure** for scalable cloud infrastructure to handle dynamic game content generation and real-time interactions.
- **Docker** for containerizing the application and ensuring consistency across environments.
- **Kubernetes** for orchestrating containerized applications, particularly for multiplayer games.

Step 3: Game Design and Core Functionality

a. Dynamic Storytelling and Dialogue System

Purpose: To create dynamic, adaptive conversations with NPCs, where each interaction with the player can shape the course of the story.

Example API Endpoint: Dialogue Generation

```python
Copy code
import openai
from flask import Flask, request, jsonify

app = Flask(__name__)

# Set OpenAI API Key
openai.api_key = "your_openai_api_key"

@app.route("/generate-dialogue", methods=["POST"])
def generate_dialogue():
    """Generate dynamic NPC dialogue based on player input."""
    data = request.json
    player_input = data.get("player_input", "")
    npc_name = data.get("npc_name", "Unknown NPC")

    # Generate dialogue using GPT-3
    response = openai.Completion.create(
        engine="davinci-codex",  # Or GPT-4, depending on complexity
        prompt=f"The player talks to {npc_name}: {player_input}\n\n{npc_name} responds:",
        max_tokens=150
    )

    # Return NPC's response
```

```python
    return jsonify({"npc_response": response.choices[0].text.strip()})
```

b. Procedural Content Generation (PCG)

Purpose: To generate game worlds, quests, and characters dynamically. Players can interact with these generated elements, and the content adapts based on their choices.

Example API Endpoint: Generate Quest
```python
python
Copy code
@app.route("/generate-quest", methods=["POST"])
def generate_quest():
    """Generate a dynamic quest for the player."""
    data = request.json
    player_level = data.get("player_level", 1)
    quest_type = data.get("quest_type", "exploration")

    # Generate quest using LLM
    prompt = f"Generate a {quest_type} quest for a player of level
{player_level}."
    response = openai.Completion.create(
        engine="davinci-codex",
        prompt=prompt,
        max_tokens=300
    )

    return jsonify({"quest_description": response.choices[0].text.strip()})
```

c. AI Dungeon Master for Tabletop Games

Purpose: The LLM-powered Dungeon Master (DM) will create dynamic encounters, NPC dialogues, and world-building elements for tabletop RPGs like Dungeons & Dragons.

Example API Endpoint: AI DM for RPG
```python
python
Copy code
@app.route("/create-rpg-encounter", methods=["POST"])
def create_rpg_encounter():
    """Generate a dynamic RPG encounter scenario."""
    data = request.json
    location = data.get("location", "forest")
    player_action = data.get("action", "explore")

    # Generate encounter using LLM
    prompt = f"The player is in a {location} and decides to {player_action}.
Describe the encounter."
    response = openai.Completion.create(
        engine="davinci-codex",
        prompt=prompt,
        max_tokens=250
    )
```

143

```
    return jsonify({"encounter_description":
response.choices[0].text.strip()})
```

d. Personalized Game Recommendations

Purpose: To recommend quests, games, or in-game content based on player preferences.

Example API Endpoint: Game Recommendation
```python
python
Copy code
@app.route("/recommend-game", methods=["POST"])
def recommend_game():
    """Recommend a game based on player interests and preferences."""
    data = request.json
    player_interests = data.get("player_interests", [])

    # Generate recommendation using LLM
    prompt = f"Based on the following interests: {',
'.join(player_interests)}, recommend a game or quest."
    response = openai.Completion.create(
        engine="davinci-codex",
        prompt=prompt,
        max_tokens=150
    )

    return jsonify({"recommendation": response.choices[0].text.strip()})
```

Step 4: Frontend Implementation

1. Dynamic Dialogue System:

- A chat interface in the game where players can interact with NPCs.
- The NPC responses are dynamically generated, allowing for branching dialogue based on previous player choices.

2. Game Progress Dashboard:

- Players can view their active quests, explore new worlds, and track game progress.
- A dynamic quest log that updates based on the quests generated by the LLM.

3. In-Game Companions:

- Players can interact with AI companions who evolve based on their relationship with the player. The companions' dialogues and actions are personalized based on the ongoing story.

Step 5: Deployment

1. **API Hosting**: Deploy the backend APIs on cloud platforms like **AWS Lambda**, **Google Cloud Functions**, or **Azure Functions** for scalability.
2. **Game Hosting**: Host the game or interactive content on platforms like **Unity Cloud**, **Steam**, or **Epic Games Store**.
3. **Model Hosting**: Host models using **Hugging Face Inference API**, **AWS SageMaker**, or **Google AI Platform** for scalable and low-latency inference.

Step 6: Scaling and Maintenance

- **Game Updates**: Continuously refine and update the game content and AI-generated interactions based on player feedback and behavior.
- **Real-Time Performance**: Optimize API calls to handle high real-time performance for multiplayer or live interactions.

Chapter No. 26 Research and Scientific Applications

Introduction:

Research and Scientific Applications using **Large Language Models (LLMs)** can enhance data analysis, research paper generation, hypothesis testing, scientific simulations, and more. These applications can process large volumes of data, provide insights, assist in literature reviews, and even generate hypotheses or draft research papers.

Here's how we can create a Research and Scientific Application using LLMs:

Step 1: Define Core Features for Research and Scientific Applications

1. Literature Review Assistant

- **Functionality**: Automatically generate summaries and insights from scientific papers, journals, or books, providing an overview of existing research in a specific field.
- **LLM Capabilities**: Extract relevant information, summarize content, and compare research findings across different papers.

2. Research Paper Generation and Assistance

- **Functionality**: Assist in drafting research papers, creating introductions, discussions, or conclusions based on the provided data and research focus.
- **LLM Capabilities**: Generate scientifically coherent paragraphs, suggest relevant references, and even provide arguments or counter-arguments.

3. Data Analysis and Visualization Helper

- **Functionality**: Help researchers analyze data sets by suggesting methods, explaining results, and even generating charts or visualizations based on the data.
- **LLM Capabilities**: Interpret data, generate code for visualizations, and provide insights based on the data trends.

4. Hypothesis Generation and Testing

- **Functionality**: Automatically generate hypotheses based on existing literature and data, or test hypotheses with statistical analysis.
- **LLM Capabilities**: Create testable hypotheses, suggest experiments, and help researchers design studies to validate or disprove them.

5. Research Idea and Problem-Solving Assistant

- **Functionality**: Provide creative ideas for new research topics, solve scientific problems, and assist researchers in framing questions based on existing scientific knowledge.
- **LLM Capabilities**: Suggest areas for further research, generate potential experiments, and help with scientific problem-solving.

6. Scientific Simulation and Modeling Assistance

- **Functionality**: Assist in building simulations, mathematical models, and interpreting simulation results.
- **LLM Capabilities**: Generate code for models, explain the results, and provide insights into model behavior or real-world applicability.

7. Automated Peer Review

- **Functionality**: Automatically review research papers for clarity, structure, logic, grammar, and scientific accuracy.
- **LLM Capabilities**: Provide peer review feedback, suggest improvements, and assess the quality of arguments or data.

8. Grant Proposal Assistance

- **Functionality**: Help researchers write compelling grant proposals, including generating drafts, budgets, and background research.
- **LLM Capabilities**: Generate grant proposal sections, including abstracts, objectives, methods, and budgets.

Step 2: Choose Technology Stack

Frontend Technologies:

- **React** or **Vue.js** for building a web-based platform where researchers can interact with the AI.
- **Django** (for Python-based) or **Flask** for backend API interaction.
- **Jupyter Notebooks** for interactive scientific work and code execution.

Backend Technologies:

- **Python** (Flask, FastAPI, Django) for API and LLM integrations.
- **Node.js** or **Go** for real-time performance, especially if multiple users are interacting simultaneously.

AI and NLP Libraries:

- **OpenAI GPT** or **Hugging Face Transformers**: Use models like GPT-4 or specialized models to generate and understand scientific content.
- **spaCy** or **NLTK**: For additional text processing, scientific entity recognition (like gene names, chemical compounds, etc.).
- **SciKit Learn** or **TensorFlow/PyTorch**: For integrating machine learning-based scientific models.

Data Processing & Visualization:

- **Pandas** for data analysis.
- **Matplotlib** and **Seaborn** for generating visualizations.
- **Plotly** or **Bokeh** for more interactive visualizations.

Deployment:

- **Docker** for containerized applications, ensuring portability.
- **Kubernetes** for managing containerized applications, particularly when scaling research projects or handling large datasets.
- **AWS**, **Google Cloud**, or **Microsoft Azure** for scalable infrastructure, storage, and real-time data processing.

Step 3: Example Features and Code Implementation

a. Literature Review Assistant

This feature helps summarize research papers, articles, or books to assist researchers in reviewing existing literature.

Example API Endpoint: Literature Review

```python
Copy code
import openai
from flask import Flask, request, jsonify

app = Flask(__name__)

# Set OpenAI API Key
openai.api_key = "your_openai_api_key"

@app.route("/summarize-paper", methods=["POST"])
def summarize_paper():
    """Summarize a research paper or article."""
    data = request.json
    paper_text = data.get("paper_text", "")

    # Generate summary using GPT
    response = openai.Completion.create(
        engine="davinci-codex",
```

```
        prompt=f"Summarize the following research paper:\n{paper_text}",
        max_tokens=500
    )

    return jsonify({"summary": response.choices[0].text.strip()})
```

b. Research Paper Generation Assistance

Researchers can receive help in drafting sections of a paper, like the introduction, literature review, or conclusion.

Example API Endpoint: Generate Paper Section

```python
Copy code
@app.route("/generate-paper-section", methods=["POST"])
def generate_paper_section():
    """Generate a section of the research paper."""
    data = request.json
    section_type = data.get("section_type", "Introduction")  # e.g.,
"Introduction", "Methods", "Conclusion"
    topic = data.get("topic", "Climate Change")

    # Generate the section of the paper using GPT
    prompt = f"Generate the {section_type} for a research paper on the topic:
{topic}."
    response = openai.Completion.create(
        engine="davinci-codex",
        prompt=prompt,
        max_tokens=300
    )

    return jsonify({"paper_section": response.choices[0].text.strip()})
```

c. Data Analysis and Visualization Helper

This feature suggests methods to analyze data and generates visualizations based on datasets.

Example API Endpoint: Data Analysis Helper

```python
Copy code
import pandas as pd
import matplotlib.pyplot as plt
from flask import Flask, request, jsonify
import io
import base64

app = Flask(__name__)

@app.route("/analyze-data", methods=["POST"])
def analyze_data():
    """Analyze scientific data and generate a visualization."""
    data = request.json
    csv_data = data.get("csv_data", "")
```

```
# Load the CSV data into a DataFrame
df = pd.read_csv(io.StringIO(csv_data))

# Simple data analysis (e.g., correlation matrix)
corr_matrix = df.corr()

# Generate a heatmap visualization
fig, ax = plt.subplots()
cax = ax.matshow(corr_matrix, cmap="coolwarm")
fig.colorbar(cax)

# Convert plot to base64 to send to client
img_io = io.BytesIO()
plt.savefig(img_io, format="png")
img_io.seek(0)
img_base64 = base64.b64encode(img_io.read()).decode("utf-8")

return jsonify({"correlation_matrix_img": img_base64})
```

d. Hypothesis Generation

This feature helps generate scientific hypotheses based on existing literature.

Example API Endpoint: Generate Hypothesis

```python
Copy code
@app.route("/generate-hypothesis", methods=["POST"])
def generate_hypothesis():
    """Generate a scientific hypothesis based on data."""
    data = request.json
    research_topic = data.get("research_topic", "Gene Mutation in Cancer")

    # Generate hypothesis using GPT
    prompt = f"Based on the research topic '{research_topic}', generate a
testable hypothesis for scientific study."
    response = openai.Completion.create(
        engine="davinci-codex",
        prompt=prompt,
        max_tokens=150
    )

    return jsonify({"hypothesis": response.choices[0].text.strip()})
```

Step 4: Frontend Implementation

1. Interactive Dashboard:

- Allow users to input scientific data, research topics, or papers for analysis.
- Display results such as data analysis, visualizations, or hypotheses generated by the LLM.

- Allow researchers to interact with the system for literature review, generating sections of research papers, etc.

2. Dynamic Literature Review:

- Display summaries, insights, or comparisons of multiple papers in a user-friendly interface.

3. Collaboration Features:

- Provide collaboration tools for team-based research, allowing multiple researchers to interact with the assistant and review or refine generated outputs.

Step 5: Deployment and Scalability

1. **API Hosting**: Use cloud services such as **AWS Lambda**, **Google Cloud Functions**, or **Azure Functions** to scale the LLM-based APIs.
2. **Data Storage**: Store research data, results, and user interactions in databases such as **MongoDB** or **PostgreSQL**.
3. **Load Balancing**: Use **Kubernetes** for scaling containerized applications, ensuring smooth interactions even with large data volumes.

152

Chapter No. 27 Accessibility Solutions Application

Introduction:

Accessibility Solutions Application using **Large Language Models (LLMs)** can be an impactful tool for improving the accessibility of digital content for individuals with disabilities. These applications can assist with text-to-speech, speech-to-text, content summarization, language translation, and more, enhancing accessibility for people with visual impairments, hearing impairments, learning disabilities, and cognitive challenges.

Here's how we can create an Accessibility Solutions Application using LLMs:

Step 1: Define Core Features for Accessibility Solutions

1. Text-to-Speech (TTS) for Visually Impaired Users

- **Functionality**: Convert written content (web pages, articles, emails) into spoken words for visually impaired or blind users.
- **LLM Capabilities**: Generate natural and clear speech with contextual understanding to maintain meaning and tone.

2. Speech-to-Text (STT) for Users with Hearing Impairments

- **Functionality**: Convert spoken language into written text for individuals who are deaf or hard of hearing.
- **LLM Capabilities**: Transcribe speech accurately with support for multiple languages and dialects, offering real-time captions.

3. Content Summarization

- **Functionality**: Automatically summarize large blocks of text into concise, digestible summaries for users with cognitive or learning disabilities.
- **LLM Capabilities**: Identify key points, remove unnecessary information, and provide a simplified version of the text.

4. Language Translation for Multilingual Accessibility

- **Functionality**: Translate content into multiple languages, including sign languages, to ensure accessibility for non-native speakers or users with diverse linguistic backgrounds.
- **LLM Capabilities**: Real-time translation of written and spoken content into various languages, including sign language interpretations.

5. Cognitive Support Assistant

- **Functionality**: Assist users with cognitive disabilities by simplifying complex language and instructions and providing contextual explanations.
- **LLM Capabilities**: Offer paraphrasing, explanations, and more accessible wording in real-time.

6. Voice Commands and Control for Hands-Free Interaction

- **Functionality**: Enable hands-free navigation of websites, applications, or devices through voice commands for users with physical disabilities.
- **LLM Capabilities**: Enable real-time voice recognition, natural language understanding, and task execution based on user instructions.

7. Personalized Accessibility Features

- **Functionality**: Adapt accessibility features based on individual preferences, disabilities, or user behaviors (e.g., font size, text contrast, voice preferences).
- **LLM Capabilities**: Personalize user experiences by adjusting content, tone, and interaction based on user needs.

8. Real-time Contextual Help

- **Functionality**: Provide real-time assistance and guidance for users struggling with navigation or understanding complex content.
- **LLM Capabilities**: Use context-based understanding to offer explanations, step-by-step guidance, and help in accessible formats.

Step 2: Choose Technology Stack

Frontend Technologies:

- **React** or **Vue.js** for building a responsive, accessible user interface that complies with accessibility standards (WCAG).
- **Django** (for Python-based) or **Flask** for backend API interaction and integration with LLM models.

Backend Technologies:

- **Python** (Flask, FastAPI) for building the API layer.
- **Node.js** or **Go** for real-time features like voice commands and STT.

AI and NLP Libraries:

- **OpenAI GPT** for general language understanding, speech generation, and summarization.
- **Google Speech-to-Text** or **Deepgram** for accurate speech recognition and transcription.
- **TTS models** (like **Tacotron 2** or **FastSpeech 2**) for text-to-speech capabilities.

- **Hugging Face Transformers** for language translation and summarization tasks.
- **spaCy** or **NLTK** for additional text processing.

Data Storage and Management:

- **MongoDB** for storing user preferences, accessibility configurations, and content data.
- **PostgreSQL** or **SQLite** for managing more structured data (e.g., user profiles).

Deployment:

- **Docker** to containerize the application for portability.
- **Kubernetes** for managing scalability, especially for real-time interactions (e.g., speech-to-text).
- **AWS**, **Google Cloud**, or **Azure** for infrastructure, with services like **AWS Polly** for text-to-speech and **Google Cloud Text-to-Speech**.

Step 3: Example Features and Code Implementation

a. Text-to-Speech (TTS) for Visually Impaired Users

Example Code for TTS using Google Cloud TTS API:

```python
Copy code
from google.cloud import texttospeech

client = texttospeech.TextToSpeechClient()

def text_to_speech(text: str, language_code: str = 'en-US'):
    synthesis_input = texttospeech.SynthesisInput(text=text)

    # Choose the voice parameters
    voice = texttospeech.VoiceSelectionParams(
        language_code=language_code,
ssml_gender=texttospeech.SsmlVoiceGender.NEUTRAL
    )

    # Set audio configuration
    audio_config = texttospeech.AudioConfig(
        audio_encoding=texttospeech.AudioEncoding.MP3
    )

    # Perform text-to-speech request
    response = client.synthesize_speech(
        input=synthesis_input, voice=voice, audio_config=audio_config
    )

    # Save the response as an audio file
    with open("output.mp3", "wb") as out:
        out.write(response.audio_content)
    print("Audio content written to file 'output.mp3'")
```

```
# Example usage
text_to_speech("Welcome to the accessibility solutions app!")
```

b. Speech-to-Text (STT) for Hearing Impaired Users

Example Code for Speech-to-Text using Google Cloud Speech-to-Text:

```python
Copy code
from google.cloud import speech

client = speech.SpeechClient()

def speech_to_text(audio_file_path: str):
    with open(audio_file_path, "rb") as audio_file:
        audio_content = audio_file.read()

    audio = speech.RecognitionAudio(content=audio_content)

    config = speech.RecognitionConfig(
        encoding=speech.RecognitionConfig.AudioEncoding.LINEAR16,
        sample_rate_hertz=16000,
        language_code="en-US",
    )

    # Perform speech-to-text request
    response = client.recognize(config=config, audio=audio)

    # Extract text from the response
    for result in response.results:
        print("Transcript: {}".format(result.alternatives[0].transcript))

# Example usage
speech_to_text("path_to_audio_file.wav")
```

c. Content Summarization

Example Code for Summarization using OpenAI GPT:

```python
Copy code
import openai

openai.api_key = "your_openai_api_key"

def summarize_text(text: str):
    response = openai.Completion.create(
        engine="text-davinci-003",
        prompt=f"Summarize the following text:\n{text}",
        max_tokens=150
    )
    return response.choices[0].text.strip()

# Example usage
long_text = """
```

```
Accessibility is a critical issue in the digital age. Many people with
disabilities struggle to use websites and applications designed without
considering accessibility standards. This results in inequality, limiting
access to information and services for individuals who are visually impaired,
hearing impaired, or have cognitive disabilities.
"""
summary = summarize_text(long_text)
print(summary)
```

d. Real-Time Contextual Help

Example Code for Contextual Help using OpenAI GPT:
```python
python
Copy code
def get_contextual_help(query: str):
    prompt = f"Provide a helpful response to the following accessibility-
related query: {query}"
    response = openai.Completion.create(
        engine="davinci-codex",
        prompt=prompt,
        max_tokens=150
    )
    return response.choices[0].text.strip()

# Example usage
help_query = "How can I adjust the font size on this website?"
help_response = get_contextual_help(help_query)
print(help_response)
```

Step 4: Frontend Implementation

1. Interactive Dashboard:

- Allow users to customize accessibility preferences (e.g., voice type, text size, high contrast mode).
- Provide real-time text-to-speech and speech-to-text features on the interface.

2. Real-Time Assistance:

- Provide users with contextual help via chat or voice commands, guiding them through any navigation or content.

3. Accessible Content:

- Ensure that content displayed on the platform adheres to accessibility guidelines, with customizable options like font size, contrast, and readable fonts.

4. Voice Control:

- Enable voice commands to navigate through content, trigger actions (e.g., reading a section aloud), and more.

Step 5: Deployment and Scalability

1. **Cloud Services**: Use **AWS**, **Google Cloud**, or **Azure** for TTS/STT API integrations and scalable hosting.
2. **Database**: Store user preferences and settings in databases like **MongoDB** or **PostgreSQL**.
3. **Real-time Interaction**: Use **WebSockets** or **Socket.io** for real-time interactions, especially for voice control or live captioning.

Chapter No. 28 Creative Applications

Introduction:

Creative Applications using **Large Language Models (LLMs)** can be a game-changer for various industries, including content creation, art, music, design, writing, and more. LLMs can assist in generating creative ideas, automating repetitive tasks, and even collaborating with human creators to push the boundaries of what's possible in creative fields.

Steps to Create a Creative Application Using LLMs

Step 1: Define Core Features for Creative Applications

1. Text Generation for Creative Writing

- **Functionality**: LLMs can generate short stories, poetry, blog posts, and other forms of creative writing based on a prompt or theme.
- **LLM Capabilities**: Write in different tones and styles, assist with brainstorming ideas, or even suggest plot twists and character developments for stories.

2. Art Generation and Concept Design

- **Functionality**: Generate visual art concepts or design ideas based on descriptions or specific themes.
- **LLM Capabilities**: Integrate with tools like **DALL·E** or **MidJourney** to create digital art, illustrations, or concept art from textual descriptions.

3. Music Composition Assistance

- **Functionality**: Create melodies, harmonies, or even entire pieces of music based on specific genres, moods, or instruments.
- **LLM Capabilities**: Use LLMs in conjunction with music composition models to suggest chord progressions, melodies, and lyrics.

4. Collaborative Brainstorming and Idea Generation

- **Functionality**: Assist creators by providing brainstorming support for projects, whether it's for a film, advertisement, product design, or any other creative work.
- **LLM Capabilities**: Suggest new concepts, merge ideas, and help expand on a given concept.

5. Interactive Storytelling

- **Functionality**: Develop interactive narratives where the user can choose their path or participate in creating the storyline, often used in video games, role-playing, or immersive experiences.
- **LLM Capabilities**: Dynamically adapt the story based on user choices, creating an ever-evolving narrative.

6. Game Development Assistance

- **Functionality**: Generate game levels, quests, dialogues, and more for game developers, helping them speed up the creative process.
- **LLM Capabilities**: Assist with procedural content generation, including creating NPC dialogues, mission designs, and world-building.

7. Creative Prompt Generators

- **Functionality**: Automatically generate creative prompts for writers, artists, musicians, or any other creatives to overcome blocks and spark inspiration.
- **LLM Capabilities**: Generate unique prompts for different forms of creative work (e.g., writing prompts, design briefs, music themes).

8. AI-Assisted Visual Design and Layout Creation

- **Functionality**: Automatically generate website layouts, advertising materials, and design mockups based on specific content or branding guidelines.
- **LLM Capabilities**: Work alongside visual design tools to suggest layouts, typography, and color schemes.

9. Video Script and Dialogue Generation

- **Functionality**: Create video scripts or dialogues for movies, YouTube videos, advertisements, etc.
- **LLM Capabilities**: Assist in writing dialogue, creating engaging video scripts, and offering creative approaches to storytelling.

Step 2: Choose Technology Stack

Frontend Technologies:

- **React** or **Vue.js** for interactive interfaces, ensuring smooth user experience.
- **Figma** or **Sketch** for design collaboration, and exporting assets for use in the application.
- **WebRTC** for real-time collaboration in creative projects, allowing multiple users to work together on tasks.

Backend Technologies:

- **Python** for handling AI interactions, especially for integration with LLM models.
- **Node.js** or **Go** for scalable backend infrastructure, especially if you plan to use real-time data or have heavy user interaction.

AI and NLP Libraries:

- **OpenAI GPT-4** for creative writing and text generation.
- **DALL·E** or **Stable Diffusion** for generating visual artwork from textual descriptions.
- **Magenta** for music composition and AI-generated melodies.
- **Hugging Face Transformers** for a variety of creative applications like text generation, summarization, and content generation.
- **RunwayML** for advanced creative tools and models for generating visuals, audio, and videos.

Data Storage and Management:

- **MongoDB** or **Firebase** for storing user-generated content, creative projects, and collaboration data.
- **AWS S3** for storing large media files like videos, images, and audio tracks.

Deployment:

- **Docker** for containerizing the application.
- **Heroku**, **AWS**, or **Google Cloud** for scalable deployment, particularly when dealing with heavy media assets or AI models.

Step 3: Example Use Case Scenarios and Code Implementation

a. Text Generation for Creative Writing (e.g., Story or Poetry)

Example Code for Text Generation using OpenAI GPT:

```python
python
Copy code
import openai

openai.api_key = "your_openai_api_key"

def generate_story_or_poetry(prompt: str):
    response = openai.Completion.create(
        engine="text-davinci-003",  # or another appropriate GPT-4 model
        prompt=prompt,
        max_tokens=200,  # Set token limit based on the desired length
        temperature=0.7,  # Adjust the creativity level (0-1)
        top_p=1,
        frequency_penalty=0,
        presence_penalty=0
```

```
    )
    return response.choices[0].text.strip()

# Example usage
prompt = "Write a short fantasy story about a dragon and a knight who become
friends."
story = generate_story_or_poetry(prompt)
print(story)
```

b. Visual Art Generation via Text-to-Image

Example Code for DALL·E (or Stable Diffusion) integration:

```python
Copy code
from openai import OpenAI

openai.api_key = "your_openai_api_key"

def generate_artwork(description: str):
    response = openai.Image.create(
        prompt=description,
        n=1,
        size="1024x1024"  # Adjust based on your requirements
    )
    return response['data'][0]['url']

# Example usage
art_description = "A futuristic city skyline with neon lights and flying
cars."
artwork_url = generate_artwork(art_description)
print(f"Generated artwork URL: {artwork_url}")
```

c. Music Composition Assistance

Example Code for Music Composition via Magenta:

```python
Copy code
import magenta
from magenta.models.performance_rnn import performance_rnn_generate
from magenta.protobuf import generator_pb2
from magenta.protobuf import music_pb2
from magenta.music import midi_io

def generate_music(seed_midi_path: str, output_path: str):
    # Load seed MIDI file
    seed_sequence = midi_io.read_midi(seed_midi_path)

    # Set up music generation parameters
    generator = performance_rnn_generate.PerformanceRnnGenerator()
    generator.initialize_from_checkpoint('path_to_checkpoint')

    # Generate music based on the seed
    generated_sequence = generator.generate(seed_sequence)
```

```
      # Write the generated sequence to an output MIDI file
      midi_io.sequence_proto_to_midi_file(generated_sequence, output_path)

# Example usage
generate_music('seed_midi_file.mid', 'output_generated_music.mid')
```

d. Interactive Storytelling for Games or Apps

Example Code for Interactive Storytelling using OpenAI GPT:

```python
Copy code
def generate_interactive_story(prompt: str, user_choice: str):
    new_prompt = f"{prompt} The user decides to {user_choice}. Continue the
story."
    response = openai.Completion.create(
        engine="text-davinci-003",
        prompt=new_prompt,
        max_tokens=150
    )
    return response.choices[0].text.strip()

# Example usage
initial_prompt = "You are an explorer in a mystical forest. You come across
an ancient temple. "
user_choice = "enter the temple"
story = generate_interactive_story(initial_prompt, user_choice)
print(story)
```

Step 4: Frontend and User Interaction

1. **Create Interactive User Interface**:
    o   **Text Generation**: Allow users to input prompts and generate stories or poems.
    o   **Art Generation**: Provide a text box where users can describe the art they want to generate, and display the generated artwork.
    o   **Music Composition**: Provide options to upload seed music files or generate compositions from scratch.
    o   **Interactive Story**: Let users make choices and interact with the storyline, dynamically adjusting the narrative.
2. **Collaboration and Sharing**:
    o   Allow users to collaborate on creative projects, invite others to contribute to stories, artworks, or music, and share the final pieces.

Step 5: Deployment and Scalability

1. **Cloud Storage**: Store user-generated content like art, music, or stories in **AWS S3** or **Google Cloud Storage**.

2. **Real-Time Collaboration**: Enable real-time editing and collaboration using **WebSockets** or **Firebase** for seamless interaction.
3. **Performance Optimization**: Ensure AI models are deployed efficiently, possibly using **GPU instances** or **cloud-based platforms** like **Google AI** for faster processing.

Chapter No. 29 Responsible AI Solutions

Introduction:

Responsible AI Solutions is crucial for ensuring that AI technologies are used ethically, fairly, and transparently. Such an application can provide features that help developers and organizations manage and deploy AI systems in a way that aligns with ethical standards, mitigates risks, and promotes fairness, transparency, and accountability.

Key Principles of Responsible AI:

1. **Fairness** – Avoiding bias and ensuring that AI systems do not unfairly disadvantage individuals or groups.
2. **Transparency** – Ensuring that the decision-making processes of AI models are understandable and explainable.
3. **Accountability** – Creating systems that hold stakeholders responsible for the outcomes of AI systems.
4. **Privacy** – Protecting user data and ensuring data is handled securely and ethically.
5. **Safety and Security** – Ensuring AI systems are robust, safe, and resilient against adversarial attacks or misuse.

Steps to Create a Responsible AI Solution Application

Step 1: Define Core Features of the Responsible AI Application

1. **Bias Detection and Mitigation**
   - **Functionality**: Detect and mitigate biases in data and AI models. This can include testing for gender, racial, or socioeconomic biases.
   - **LLM Capabilities**: Use LLMs to analyze and provide recommendations for fairness improvements by auditing models and data pipelines.
2. **Model Explainability**
   - **Functionality**: Provide tools to explain AI models' predictions, such as feature importance, decision paths, and reasoning behind decisions.
   - **LLM Capabilities**: Use models like **SHAP** or **LIME** for explainability and generate human-readable explanations for complex AI models, enhancing transparency.
3. **Adversarial Testing and Robustness**
   - **Functionality**: Test AI models for robustness against adversarial attacks, ensuring they perform well under different conditions.
   - **LLM Capabilities**: Use LLMs to identify vulnerabilities and suggest defenses against adversarial manipulation.

4. **Data Privacy and Protection**
   - o **Functionality**: Implement features to ensure that user data is collected, processed, and stored securely, following privacy laws such as GDPR and CCPA.
   - o **LLM Capabilities**: Generate privacy guidelines and recommendations for handling sensitive data, ensuring compliance with regulations.
5. **AI Ethics Audits**
   - o **Functionality**: Conduct regular audits of AI models and applications to ensure that ethical guidelines are being followed.
   - o **LLM Capabilities**: Use LLMs to scan documentation and AI models to assess their ethical alignment and provide suggestions for improvement.
6. **Regulatory Compliance Monitoring**
   - o **Functionality**: Track changes in AI regulations and ensure compliance with evolving legal and ethical standards.
   - o **LLM Capabilities**: Use LLMs to automatically track regulations and interpret them to provide actionable insights for development teams.
7. **Transparency Reports Generation**
   - o **Functionality**: Generate regular reports that provide transparency about AI model operations, decisions, and metrics to stakeholders.
   - o **LLM Capabilities**: Automate the creation of detailed, human-readable reports that summarize key performance, fairness, and ethics metrics for AI systems.

Step 2: Choose the Technology Stack

Frontend Technologies:

- **React** or **Vue.js** for dynamic user interfaces that allow developers and stakeholders to interact with AI models, review fairness metrics, and generate reports.
- **D3.js** or **Plotly** for visualizations of model predictions, fairness analysis, and ethical audits.

Backend Technologies:

- **Python**: For integrating AI ethics algorithms, model explainability tools, and fairness audits.
- **Flask** or **Django** for building a RESTful API to serve AI model assessments and audits.

AI and NLP Libraries:

- **SHAP** or **LIME** for model explainability and transparency.
- **Fairlearn** or **AI Fairness 360** (from IBM) for fairness assessments and bias detection in AI models.
- **PyTorch** or **TensorFlow** for building and training AI models with integrated fairness considerations.
- **Hugging Face Transformers** for integrating NLP models with responsible AI tools.

Security and Privacy Tools:

- **PySyft** for implementing privacy-preserving techniques like Federated Learning and Differential Privacy.
- **Cryptography Libraries** like **PyCryptodome** for secure data storage and communication.

Regulatory Compliance:

- **GDPR Compliance Libraries** for ensuring data privacy (e.g., **GDPR Python**).
- **Compliance as a Service** tools to automate compliance checks and ensure ongoing monitoring.

Step 3: Key Application Features and Code Implementation

1. Bias Detection and Mitigation

Example Code for Bias Detection using Fairlearn:

```python
python
Copy code
from fairlearn.metrics import MetricFrame, false_positive_rate,
false_negative_rate
from fairlearn.reductions import ExponentiatedGradient, DemographicParity
from sklearn.metrics import accuracy_score

# Sample data: model predictions, true labels, and sensitive attribute (e.g.,
gender)
predictions = [1, 0, 1, 1, 0]
labels = [1, 0, 1, 1, 0]
sensitive_attribute = [0, 1, 0, 1, 1]   # 0 = male, 1 = female

# Calculate fairness metrics
metric_frame = MetricFrame(metrics={"accuracy": accuracy_score,
"false_positive_rate": false_positive_rate},
                           y_true=labels,
                           y_pred=predictions,
                           sensitive_features=sensitive_attribute)
print(metric_frame)

# Bias mitigation example: applying Exponentiated Gradient to reduce bias
# (This assumes a pre-trained model)
mitigator = ExponentiatedGradient(DemographicParity())
mitigator.fit(model, sensitive_features=sensitive_attribute, labels=labels)
```

2. Model Explainability (SHAP)

Example Code for SHAP (Shapley Values):

```python
python
Copy code
import shap
import xgboost as xgb
from sklearn.datasets import load_boston
import matplotlib.pyplot as plt
```

```python
# Load data and model
data = load_boston()
X = data.data
y = data.target
model = xgb.XGBRegressor().fit(X, y)

# Create SHAP explainer
explainer = shap.TreeExplainer(model)
shap_values = explainer.shap_values(X)

# Visualize feature importance
shap.summary_plot(shap_values, X)
```

3. Privacy Compliance and Data Anonymization

Example Code for Differential Privacy:
```python
python
Copy code
from tensorflow_privacy import DPQuery
from tensorflow_privacy.privacy.analysis import compute_dp_sgd_privacy

# Define differential privacy mechanism
dp_query = DPQuery(epsilon=0.5, delta=1e-5)

# Compute privacy budget
privacy_budget = compute_dp_sgd_privacy.compute_dp_sgd_privacy(n=10000,
batch_size=64, noise_multiplier=1.1, epochs=10)
print(f"Privacy budget: {privacy_budget}")
```

4. Transparency Report Generation (Using LLMs)

Example Code to Generate Reports using OpenAI GPT:
```python
python
Copy code
import openai

openai.api_key = "your_openai_api_key"

def generate_transparency_report(ai_model_metrics):
    prompt = f"Generate a transparency report for an AI model with the
following metrics: {ai_model_metrics}. Include explanations about fairness,
accuracy, and safety."
    response = openai.Completion.create(
        engine="text-davinci-003",
        prompt=prompt,
        max_tokens=500
    )
    return response.choices[0].text.strip()

# Example usage
ai_model_metrics = {"accuracy": 0.85, "bias_score": 0.15,
"privacy_compliance": "GDPR"}
report = generate_transparency_report(ai_model_metrics)
```

Step 4: Frontend User Interface

1. **Dashboard**:
   - o **Model Audit Summary**: A visual dashboard displaying AI model performance metrics, fairness analysis, and potential risks.
   - o **Bias and Fairness Metrics**: Graphs and visualizations highlighting any detected biases in the model (e.g., performance differences across demographic groups).
   - o **Explainability Section**: Allow users to interact with the model to see how specific inputs affect predictions.
   - o **Privacy Compliance Status**: Display compliance status for regulations like GDPR, HIPAA, etc.
   - o **Transparency Reports**: Allow users to generate and download detailed reports.
2. **Real-Time Collaboration**:
   - o Allow multiple users (data scientists, engineers, compliance officers) to collaborate on responsible AI audits, suggesting improvements, and reviewing results.

Step 5: Deployment and Monitoring

1. **Cloud Deployment**: Deploy the application using services like **AWS**, **Azure**, or **Google Cloud** to scale efficiently.
2. **Monitoring**: Implement real-time monitoring tools to assess the performance of deployed AI models, track any changes in fairness or transparency, and ensure compliance with updated regulations.
3. **User Feedback**: Collect feedback from users to continuously improve the responsible AI features and tools.

Chapter No. 30 Emerging Use Cases

Introduction:

Emerging Use Cases with Large Language Models (LLMs) is an exciting challenge because it involves building tools that can push the boundaries of AI capabilities. These use cases often require highly innovative approaches and combine multiple advanced AI techniques like NLP, computer vision, reinforcement learning, and multimodal interaction.

Key Principles for Emerging Use Cases:

1. **Flexibility** – The application should be adaptable to new problems as they emerge.
2. **Interdisciplinary Integration** – It should combine various AI technologies such as NLP, computer vision, robotics, etc., to solve complex, multi-faceted problems.
3. **Scalability** – Ensure the app can scale to handle large datasets, real-time processing, and growing user demand.
4. **User-Centric Design** – Focus on ease of use, empowering non-technical users to leverage emerging AI technologies.

Step 1: Define Key Emerging Use Cases for the Application

1. **Augmented Reality (AR) with NLP Integration**
   - **Use Case**: Create an AR platform that allows users to interact with physical environments using natural language, for example, providing contextual information about objects, locations, or people.
   - **LLM Application**: Use LLMs to interpret user queries in natural language and provide intelligent responses related to the environment in real time.
2. **AI for Creativity and Content Creation**
   - **Use Case**: Generate new types of media, such as interactive stories, music, videos, or animations, by combining LLMs with creative AI algorithms (e.g., GANs or StyleGANs).
   - **LLM Application**: Use LLMs to generate scripts, dialogues, and plots that can be further enriched by AI-driven visuals or music.
3. **Human-Machine Collaboration for Design and Prototyping**
   - **Use Case**: Build an application where LLMs help users create designs, prototypes, or plans for products, engineering solutions, or art by interpreting user input and suggesting improvements.
   - **LLM Application**: LLMs help generate concepts, suggest enhancements, and provide feedback on user designs.
4. **AI-Powered Robotics and Automation**
   - **Use Case**: Enable robots or drones to perform complex tasks like delivery, construction, or healthcare assistance using natural language commands combined with computer vision and decision-making algorithms.
   - **LLM Application**: Integrate LLMs with robotics to interpret user commands and make real-time decisions based on contextual data and environmental factors.

5. **AI for Real-time Video Analysis**
   - o **Use Case**: Build a system for real-time video analysis that can detect and interpret human behavior, emotions, or objects for applications in security, customer service, or entertainment.
   - o **LLM Application**: Use LLMs to analyze context and describe what's happening in videos in natural language, combining computer vision with NLP.

6. **Virtual Metaverse Assistants**
   - o **Use Case**: Create virtual assistants that interact with users in the metaverse, assisting them in navigating virtual spaces, finding resources, and connecting with other users.
   - o **LLM Application**: Use LLMs for dynamic conversations, helping users understand and navigate the metaverse with personalized advice.

7. **AI-Driven Healthcare Diagnostics and Personalized Treatment**
   - o **Use Case**: Build an AI system that combines medical data (e.g., images, lab reports, and symptoms) to provide real-time diagnostic suggestions and personalized treatment plans.
   - o **LLM Application**: LLMs analyze patient history, symptoms, and reports to suggest potential diagnoses and treatments, integrated with machine learning models for predictive analytics.

8. **Sentiment and Emotion Analysis for Marketing and Customer Service**
   - o **Use Case**: Develop an application that can analyze customer feedback, social media posts, or customer service interactions to gauge public sentiment or identify emotional triggers.
   - o **LLM Application**: Use LLMs to perform sentiment analysis and provide insights into customer satisfaction and emotions.

Step 2: Select Core Technologies and Libraries

Core Technologies:

- **Frontend Technologies**: React.js, Three.js (for AR/VR), WebGL (for rendering), D3.js (for data visualization).
- **Backend Technologies**: Python (Flask/Django), Node.js for scalability, WebSocket for real-time communication.
- **Machine Learning Libraries**: TensorFlow, PyTorch, Hugging Face Transformers, OpenCV (for computer vision).
- **AR/VR Frameworks**: Unity, ARCore, ARKit, Vuforia for AR/VR capabilities.
- **Cloud Platforms**: AWS, Google Cloud, or Azure for scalability and deployment.
- **Robotics Frameworks**: ROS (Robot Operating System), OpenAI Gym (for training robotic models).

AI and NLP Libraries:

- **Hugging Face Transformers**: For building LLM-based conversational agents and generative models.

- **spaCy, NLTK**: For advanced NLP processing, including entity recognition, sentiment analysis, and summarization.
- **OpenCV**: For real-time video processing and object recognition.
- **PyTorch**: For training AI models like reinforcement learning agents for robotics.
- **TensorFlow Lite**: For deploying AI models on edge devices (robots, drones, AR devices).

Step 3: Core Features and Code Examples for Emerging Use Cases

1. Augmented Reality with NLP Integration

- **Objective**: Allow users to interact with the environment using natural language and get contextual information.
- **Core Technologies**: ARKit/ARCore, Hugging Face Transformers, Unity for AR.

Example Code Snippet for AR + NLP:

```python
Copy code
import openai
import ARKit
import cv2

openai.api_key = "your_openai_api_key"

def process_user_input(user_input):
    # Use GPT to generate response to user input
    prompt = f"Provide contextual information about this location: {user_input}"
    response = openai.Completion.create(engine="text-davinci-003", prompt=prompt, max_tokens=150)
    return response.choices[0].text.strip()

def ar_object_detection(frame):
    # Detect objects in the real world using ARKit or OpenCV
    detected_objects = detect_objects_with_ar(frame)  # Simplified
    return detected_objects

def interact_with_ar_system(user_input, camera_frame):
    detected_objects = ar_object_detection(camera_frame)
    context_info = process_user_input(user_input)
    return detected_objects, context_info
```

2. AI for Creativity and Content Creation

- **Objective**: Use LLMs to generate creative writing, dialogue, or scripts.
- **Core Technologies**: GPT-3, OpenAI Codex, Hugging Face.

Example Code Snippet for Script Generation:

```python
Copy code
```

```python
import openai

openai.api_key = "your_openai_api_key"

def generate_script(prompt):
    # Generate creative script with GPT-3
    response = openai.Completion.create(
        engine="text-davinci-003",
        prompt=prompt,
        max_tokens=500
    )
    return response.choices[0].text.strip()

# Example usage
script_prompt = "Write a script for a sci-fi movie where AI becomes sentient."
script = generate_script(script_prompt)
print(script)
```

3. AI for Healthcare Diagnostics

- **Objective**: Use LLMs to analyze medical data and provide diagnostic suggestions.
- **Core Technologies**: LLMs, TensorFlow, PyTorch.

Example Code Snippet for Healthcare Diagnosis:
python
Copy code
```python
import openai

openai.api_key = "your_openai_api_key"

def analyze_medical_data(symptoms, test_results):
    # Combine user symptoms and test results to generate diagnostic suggestions
    prompt = f"Given the symptoms {symptoms} and test results {test_results}, what are the potential diagnoses?"
    response = openai.Completion.create(engine="text-davinci-003", prompt=prompt, max_tokens=200)
    return response.choices[0].text.strip()

# Example usage
symptoms = "fever, cough, fatigue"
test_results = "Positive for flu virus"
diagnosis = analyze_medical_data(symptoms, test_results)
print(diagnosis)
```

4. AI for Real-time Video Analysis

- **Objective**: Analyze video data to detect emotions or specific events.
- **Core Technologies**: OpenCV, LLMs, TensorFlow.

Example Code Snippet for Emotion Analysis in Video:
python
Copy code

```
import cv2
import openai

openai.api_key = "your_openai_api_key"

def detect_faces_in_video(video_path):
    # Use OpenCV to detect faces in a video
    video = cv2.VideoCapture(video_path)
    faces = []
    while video.isOpened():
        ret, frame = video.read()
        if not ret:
            break
        # Detect faces (simplified)
        detected_faces = detect_faces(frame)
        faces.extend(detected_faces)
    video.release()
    return faces

def analyze_video_emotion(faces):
    # Use LLM to interpret emotions from facial expressions
    prompt = f"Analyze the emotions of these faces: {faces}"
    response = openai.Completion.create(engine="text-davinci-003",
prompt=prompt, max_tokens=150)
    return response.choices[0].text.strip()

# Example usage
faces = detect_faces_in_video("sample_video.mp4")
emotion = analyze_video_emotion(faces)
print(emotion)
```

Step 4: Deployment and Monitoring

1. **Cloud Deployment**: Use scalable cloud platforms like AWS, Google Cloud, or Azure to deploy your application. For real-time applications like video analysis or robotics, ensure low-latency edge deployment.
2. **Monitoring**: Implement real-time monitoring using cloud services (e.g., AWS CloudWatch, Google Cloud Monitoring) to track performance, error logs, and user activity.
3. **User Feedback**: Continuously collect feedback from users to iterate on emerging use cases and improve the app's functionalities.

www.ingramcontent.com/pod-product-compliance
Lightning Source LLC
Chambersburg PA
CBHW080416060326
40689CB00019B/4267